A Cowgirl Remembers When...

A Cowgirl Remembers When...

Dawn Nelson

Gray Dog Press
Spokane, Washington

Gray Dog Press

For information:
Gray Dog Press, 2727 S. Mt. Vernon #4
Spokane, Washington 99223

www.GrayDogPress.com

Layout, design and editing:
Russel Davis

ISBN: 978-0-9822743-4-7
Library of Congress Control No.: 2009927312

Dedication

I dedicate these stories to two of the most
influential people of my life, who taught
me to love the land and everything
that it produces.

To my Father, Jim Singer
1951 ~ 2010
and
To my Grandfather, Pete Singer
1914 ~ 2006

Table of Contents

The Wild Child

The Horses

The Rest

Introduction

Growing up backwoods, as everybody puts it, wasn't so bad. In fact, I loved my childhood. It is the one thing I wish I could do; go back and relive it. I don't remember one thing about growing up that I didn't like.

I grew up as wild and as free on my mountain as if I were a deer or bird. I never missed out on the greater things in life, because, to me, there was nothing greater than living in my own little piece of heaven. It's funny how the land and the cattle get into your blood.

I grew up on a cattle ranch nestled snuggly between Canada and thirty thousand acres of forest service land. The border didn't stop me from crossing it back then, however, with all the security these days I am not sure I would try it any more.

I met my first best friend, Bee, when I was about two. She and I were inseparable. She was my grandpa's horse. We fell in love instantly. We went everywhere together. She got me from one mountain range to another and the one after that. She was my will, my wings, and my reason to soar.

I have a few friends who grew up ten miles to the south. Their childhood stories consisted mostly of sneaking out of the house and making out with boys. A few of them have sat before a typewriter or computer and tried as I am to jot down a few memories. To their surprise, all of their exciting stories involve me and my mountain or Old Bee.

So with urging from most of them I will sit down with pen in hand and jot down some adventures from my very own life.

I have found that over the years more and more people look at me a little peculiarly when I tell them one of the stories of my youth. They can't believe my parents raised me to be so wild in these modern times.

Some people have to travel the world to find a story that will keep people in their seats. I spent twenty some odd years and counting in my home the mountains. I have stories that are probably still some of the greatest unsolved mysteries.

I went from being a wild youth to being a wild teen and an even wilder adult. There was no place that was off limits or forbidden to me. I was never afraid to speak my mind or say something that needed to be said, no matter the situation.

I would often take to the mountains for days or weeks at a time through the summer months. During these months I learned more about surviving and staying alert to the sounds of the mountains than I could ever use in a lifetime.

In these few short stories I wrote down, I hope that you to will enjoy my youth as much as I did. If a smile creases your face even a little then I have conquered yet another goal in life.

The Wild Child

Crazy Ladies and California Boys

I call her crazy because that's what she was, however, the lady part, I am not so sure about. She did have five kids running around so I think it's a safe bet. She lived in a canyon next to a very cold creek, which everyone says was her only way of bathing. After the first time I met her, I would have to agree.

Though not very tall and barely weighing in at a hundred pounds. I am sure with all the dirt and grime she had to weigh one eighty (rough estimate).

She looked older than one of my grandpa's old saddle blankets, and used just as hard. She owned more sheep than sense or soap, but she seemed nice enough to talk to. I just figured that no one gave her a chance. So I always made sure to go out of my way to say "Hi" or talk to her a bit, all the while staying upwind.

One of my first outside jobs involved hunting a cougar for her when I was about twelve-years-old. She had been losing sheep and was beside herself with what to do. So I was hired to set up my tree-stand out in the sheep pasture with my uncle's night vision goggles to see if I could shoot him before he killed any more sheep.

She said, this cougar was a reincarnation of someone she knew who had always gone out of their way to hurt or torment her. This person had recently died so she knew it was her come back to hurt her the only way she could, by eating her sheep.

Well, as we all know, about our early teens is when little boys and little girls start to notice each other, and it was no difference for this little back woods cowgirl. Only problem was I wasn't sure what a date consisted of, until after one cold night in May.

He was from California. That was the first problem I remember having with him. I was assured by all my friends that if I dated him it would be a good thing, since everybody wished he would ask them out, it would make me more popular. I wasn't unpopular, but by no way or means did I hang out with the Barbie girls who were the most popular girls my age.

Second problem was he was blond with brown eyes and I happened, even then, to love dark hair and light blue eyes. Then again, when you're twelve and he's two years older than you, you just feel privileged to be asked. So, I said, "Yes."

Looking back on it now, I know why my Dad found it necessary to sharpen his knife when he showed up at the door in a jacket and slacks. Smelling from whatever he rolled in before he left home, he called it "Fire 'n Ice," I called it stinky.

I was so sure when he asked me the day before where I wanted to go on our date and I said, "Dress very casual," it was a surprise. Well, he stunk so bad I knew we weren't going to be able to sneak around anywhere with him smelling like that. I gave him a pair of my older brother's sweatpants to put on, a sweatshirt and a washcloth to get some of the stench off.

After some pretty strange looks, and a few I am not quite sure they classify as decent, he changed. Now I look back and find my Dad's last words of wisdom before we left to be hilarious at the least.

"Be careful and try not to scare him too much, you know how them city boys are." At the time, I was embarrassed by those few little words.

Well after that we were off and in a little over seven miles we were there. First he was shocked at the fact that I knew how to drive, and even more shocked at the fact that Mom and Dad let me drive down the main road with a gun in my back window when I was twelve. Heck, I had been driving since I was old enough to reach the pedals. As for the gun, I don't remember ever driving with out one; you never know when you might see a coyote.

By this time I am sure he thought I was absolutely crazy or at least half a heathen. Then again, maybe he thought I was driving him to some quiet spot to make all his fourteen-year-old dreams a reality.

Well according to my first grade teacher's opinion I was an absolute heathen. As for his dreams coming true, it was more like I was going to give him a reason to need therapy for most of his adult life.

When we finally got there I got the gun, goggles and a few extra bullets out of the truck just in case. That might have been the moment he realized he had no clue what I considered a first date.

By the time we walked up to Crazy Lady's front door he was already complaining about the smell and just complaining in general.

Looking back now I probably should have just turned around and drove him back to his California tie-dyed Mommy ways. But, then I would have missed the look on his face when Crazy Lady opened the door with a baby lamb covered in chicken blood and a collar around his neck.

After tying a piece of heavy twine to the collar and wishing us lots of luck the door was again closed and we stood in complete darkness. I handed him the end of the twine so he could lead the lamb. It was a cool night and the moon was bright enough to see our way down to the tree stand, but still he complained about no light. I tried to explain that we had to be quiet and stealthy. So still dumb on behalf of what we were doing he played GI Joe behind me as we walked down to the tree-stand.

Once there, I told him to climb up in the stand and sit on the left side because I am right handed. I took the lamb and tied him about a hundred yards away in a little meadow. The lamb didn't like to be left so he immediately started to bleat. I scurried up the tree and into position to await the reincarnated enemy of Crazy Lady.

With gun in hand and night vision goggles in place and lamb tied securely below, one would think California would have figured out we were hunting something by this time.

Guess again, men will be men and boys will always be boys. He still thought we were up there in that stand to turn him on. A hand on my leg brought a quick elbow to his side hard enough to knock any romantic thoughts right out of him and off the edge of the tree stand.

We sat in silence for close to three hours. Finally I caught a glimpse of what I had come to find, lerking on the edge of the meadow was the unmistakable form of a cougar.

I lowered my nightvision goggles to see if I could see him with out them, I could, as I raised my grandma's old 25-35 with open sights up to aim he crept slowly closer to the baby lamb. I aimed carefully and, KABAM! In two seconds my popular life, as we know it, came to an end.

A blood curdling scream split the air. Then all was still, not a bird in the thicket made a sound not even the lamb dared a bleat.

It seems that in those three hours of silence California had fallen asleep only to be awaken by a shot not more than five inches from his ear. Now I am not without a heart, I can see how one might be startled. Nevertheless, what came next was way beyond startled; it was plain idiotic.

He started cussing and screaming words that I won't repeat. Telling me I was a killer. Me trying to tell him that I actually just killed the killer was useless.

He stormed down that tree with all the gumption of a fox in the hen house. I told him that I lost sight of the cat after he screamed, so he might want to climb back up there for an hour or so just in case he hadn't died yet.

"A cat?" he screamed, "Who's afraid of a stupid cat? I can't believe you shot a cat!" Where he was from he said they love cats and pet them not shoot them.

Great, now he thought I shot Garfield, not a cougar. "No," I reassured him, "Not a house cat, a cougar." He was back up that tree in less than a second, shaking like a leaf and still yelling and cussing at me.

Some of what I could make out was "crazy, psycho lady" who nobody will ever date again and he would make sure of it. I agreed with him, Crazy Lady probably would never date again, but what did it have to do with him. Maybe he liked her. Well she did have five kids, maybe there was something appealing about her after all.

After about an hour I climbed down and collected the lamb. I figured I would come back tomorrow in the light to find the cat.

I went to hand California the end of the twine to lead the lamb and he freaked out again, saying some of the same things.

Well, I sure as heck wasn't handing him the gun shaking like he was. I led the lamb and carried the gun and all the other tricks of my trade.

After giving the lamb back so it could go take a bath and telling my story as casually as possible to Crazy Lady, we climbed back in the truck and headed back to my place.

The whole trip I laughed at him screaming like a girl and freaking out. I thought it was funny, he never laughed.

Back in the comfort of our living room I retold the story to my half-asleep parents. California never said a word he just looked around the room. I guessed he was just admiring my Dad's horns, antlers and hides that decorated our house.

When his Mom showed up to get him he raced out with out saying a word. At the time, I never thought anything of it. The next morning, before school, I got going early in the morning to receive and tag my kill. Later I found a whole new scene at school.

Everybody looked at me like I was contagious or something, laughs and giggles followed in my wake.

Finally a group of popular girls came up and started in about how I tried to kill California and how I would never have a chance to ever be like them.

It seems California had went to school telling everybody how "backwoods" I was and that no one in their right mind would ever date me.

If only California could see me know I am married to a real civilized cattle rancher who has done his best these past years to get as much hillbilly out of me as possible. He taught me about hunting seasons and laws. He tells me that our daughter will not grow up like I did, but he still lets me hunt as much as I want.

I do agree with one thing he tells me, our daughter won't grow up like me.

Because by the time she is five she will have one of those nifty night vision scopes for her gun and I will shoot any California boy who steps foot on my front porch.

The Midnight Ride

This is one of those stories that you laugh at now, but you didn't think it was so funny back then.

I was twelve years old when my parents had just got a new horse. She was white with black mane, tail and legs. I thought she looked like a ghost horse so I named her Stranger (don't ask).

It was a dark and stormy June night lightning seemed to flash every ten minutes or so and the rain was pouring down. A friend of mine was staying the night and we wanted to go out riding. Mom and Dad told us we couldn't go because it was dark outside, like we couldn't tell or something. We said, "All right," and headed off to bed, at least that's what they thought. Once in the bedroom we dressed in black grabbed some white bed sheets and climbed out of the window.

My friend and I decided we were going to ride bareback and for some reason or another we were going to put glow-in-the-dark paint all over our horses, tie sheets around our shoulders and run down the road in front of our neighbor's house as fast as we could, moaning and wailing. We were sure he would think we were ghosts and be afraid.

After getting Stranger and Aunt Bee from the pasture we spent close to an hour putting glow-in-the-dark paint all over them and our faces and practiced our wailing. All the while laughing and giggling about how much we were going to scare him.

We tied the sheets around our shoulders and jumped aboard our flying ghost. Down the road we flew, "Oooooohhhhhhaaaaahhhh," we moaned. We knew it had to look scary and sound horrific at most.

Past his house we galloped the poor mournful ghosts of some past dead horsemen who died a horrible death at the hands of a lynch mob most likely.

An outside light came on at his house. We moaned and wailed louder. Oh, he had to be quaking at two spooks back from the dead astride their glowing horses. Any spook would tell you that you don't haunt on a rainy night with lightning lighting up everything.

We looked great as we turned around and headed back by. Our sheets flaying out behind us, our horses and our faces glowing in the dark, the thud thud thud as our horse's hoofs hit the ground.

We moaned and wailed and the lightning was lighting everything up around us.

We moaned and we screamed,

"Oooooooooooo,aaaaaaaaaahhhhhhh....

OOOOOOooooooooo,AAAaaaaaaahhhhhh."

We turned back up towards our haystack and ran out through the field to the top of a cliff that overlooked our neighbor's house.

For the first time we noticed there must have been some twenty or more cars parked in the driveway. Everybody was standing out underneath the yard light looking around.

We could just about see the look of confusion on their faces. Not to mention the beers in their hands, they were drunk, the whole blasted crowd was blitzed. We wasted a great prank on a bunch of drunks!

Suddenly a strike of lightning lit up the sky behind us, and we heard voices yell, "There, up on the cliff." We smiled to ourselves. We did it, we got everybody's attention. Boy howdy, were we going to have a funny story to tell at school Monday.

Suddenly, there was a loud bang; man, the thunder was getting close. A bullet whizzed by my head, I swore I could hear it hit the tree behind me. Oh shoot, he was shooting at us! Who shoots at ghosts?

We shedded the sheets and ran for home. Stopping only to put the horses in their pasture. We made it back to the house that night in about two seconds.

After climbing back into my bedroom we made a vow that we would never do that again, and if we did we wouldn't stand atop the cliff to see how everything went.

Moral of the story: if you're a mortal ghost, just remember, you are not immortal.

Our Unsolved Mystery

As with most small towns, everyone has it's scary tale or folklore, but mine really happened to me and two of my friends. I was fourteen that summer and I had my first real paying job; helping Mom at our local town store stocking shelves. I wanted to quit my job for the summer so I could play and be free all summer but Mom said, "I had to learn responsibility."

"Besides," she said "you only work two days a week for a couple hours a day. How much more playing could you possibly get with only a few more hours a week?" What does she know? With an imagination like mine there might have been a need for an army scout or wild indians attacking a wagon train, you just never could tell. But she wouldn't let me quit.

Dawn Nelson

So my days went on like clockwork for a most of the summer. Every Monday and Wednesday at eight am, show up at the store, stock shelves and unload items until ten-thirty, punch out, go jump in Dad's feed truck, pick up Kristen and Jennifer and head to the river for a day in the sun until about four o'clock when we would go haul hay for Dad. Then, after dark, we would sneak into the bar in town and play pool against the drunks, often making good money.

Well, one night in June, while we were all down playing pool, a middle aged guy came in and started flirting with us. It was nasty to say the least but with fifty bucks on the table we put up with it long enough to win. After sinking the eight ball and collecting my money I turned to Jenn and asked if she was ready to get out of there. "Sure am," she said. Kristen agreed and we turned to go hang up our pool sticks.

"Wait a minute," the guy said as he grabbed my arm. "You aren't going anywhere with my money."

"Hey buddy, let go of me or you'll be sorry" I said with as much viciousness as I could muster.

"What'll you do, little lady" He slithered

"This!" I yelled as I brought the pool stick up between his legs. He wavered a little but regained his balance. So like they taught me in softball, I brought the pool stick up along side his head, WHACK! Home run! It was a loud noise and he stood there and then just fell over.

"Run!" I yelled. We all three lit out of there and jumped in the pickup with two guys right on our tail.

"You killed him!" Kristen exclaimed once we were at speeds well past getting away.

"Naw, she just whacked him," Jenn said.

We turned onto a back road and turned off our headlights and drove a few more miles in the dark. We were sure the cops were out looking for us they probably had our shirts already engraved with our name and number, but no cops ever drove by or came to the house that night. We slept in the top of the hay barn so that we could escape quick if we had to, we didn't want my parents to be accomplises to our crime.

The next day, I showed up at work a little leery but I was there just the same. The morning went as usual until about nine-fifteen when the cashier came into the cooler you could tell she was freaked out. She told me I needed to sneak out the back door and go home as quickly as possible. She said a guy was asking about me he, said he was going to get me and wanted to know where I lived.

I asked what he looked like and she described the man from the night before. So I snuck out the back door and into my Dad's truck and picked up Kristen on the way home. We were so freaked out we decided to go for a long ride on the horses to clear our heads.

We were heading down the road towards the swimming hole when a blue pickup pulled up behind us. When we realized who it was, we took off running. He sped up and pulled along side of us. We both stopped and turned around, he did the same all the while screaming profanities at us. We had nowhere to run but down the highway. It was about a half of a mile until we had a place we could get off the road. He drove up beside us and swerved over. We both jumped in the river and swam our horses toward the other side.

Freaked out didn't even come close to explaining what we were. Once back home, we told my parents what happened. They called the police and told them. A few days later a cop showed up at our door. It was a good thing it wasn't an emergency or something.

He asked us to identify him and so we went through photos and, amazingly enough, found him. After some pretty weird looks from the officer we were told to carry a gun and stay as far away from him as possible. Our imaginations ran wild...a police officer told two teenage girls to carry a gun. We knew he was a bad guy.

We guessed he was probably wanted in seven states for murder but they hadn't been able to prove anything (but they knew he did it of course) and just as they got close to getting him he would up and disappear. Of course, reappearing where some murder had just taken place. Unfortunately, we weren't far off.

A friend of the family who was a police officer told my parents that the guy had called the station claiming to have found a bracelet of a girl who had gone missing in California. He said, "When they went to get the bracelet the man had evacuated the house and left the bracelet on the doorstep. It was confirmed to have belonged to a young girl who had gone missing a few years back in California."

However, her body had been found not too long beforehand and, among numerous other things that had been done to her, she had been brutally murdered.

Our friend also told us that they were looking for the guy now trying to link him to a skeleton that had been found right down the road from our place on the edge of his property. They said the police weren't releasing any info on that yet though, because, they were afraid they might scare him away again.

My Mom decided I wasn't to go back to work again that summer and I was going to carry a pistol with me, and the three of us were not allowed to go anywhere alone. (Not that it bothered us that we had to spend the summer together.) So our summer went pretty normal except the part of having to tuck a pistol in to my swimming suit, it really didn't match the outfit.

Everywhere we went it seemed he was their watching us from afar, asking my other friends about us following us home at night even showing up at summer softball games and rodeos. He seemed to be everywhere we were. Two more bodies were found on his property that summer and another found not to far from there.

Then, all at once, he stopped following us. We didn't see that danged blue pickup or hear even a peep about him. About two weeks later our friend, the police officer, showed up and asked the three of us if we knew anything about an accident that occurred.

It seems he drove his pickup off a cliff and after investigating they concluded someone had cut his brake lines. And the most hilarious part of this story is that even to this day certain people believe that the three of us did it. I am glad to inform you that this is one crime we did not commit. But had we thought of it???

The Shoot Out

For as mean and ornery to each other as my brother and I were. Looking back now I would have to say our parents only made one real mistake in raising us, as I see it.

That was on Christmas morning when I was twelve. My brother and I awoke to find two big long packages under the Christmas tree. The tag said, "From Santa." As we ripped open the packages, we each found a genuine Red Rider BB Gun and in another, smaller, package a whole box of BBs.

We shot everything, even each other. I can't tell you how bad it hurts to get shot with a BB gun when it is pumped up as far as you can pump it on a cold winter morning. I'm not sure anything hurts more than getting shot in the fingers with a BB when your fingers are frozen.

We played BB gun wars all winter while feeding and checking cows. I seemed to always take the worst of the wars, however, being four years younger but I got in some good shots every now and then.

About January, my brother broke his BB gun while falling off the haystack. Mine was the only good working BB gun left, so he tried to steal it from me every chance he got. Finally, I had an equal playing field in our BB gun wars. His still shot but you had to pull the trigger about five times before it would shoot.

I would wake up at four o'clock in the morning just to get my BB gun first. Then, if I was lucky, he didn't beat me up and steal it from me. I had the upper hand for a morning and believe me I used it to my full advantage.

Most of the days, I ended up with his broken gun and he with my good working one. I can't tell you how many times my Mom threatened to take our guns from us if we shot each other one more time. She even did a few times but we had a small house and she had one hiding place, and we knew where it was.

I ended up with glasses by the end of January and I hated them, but Mom made me wear them and I had to thank her. On the third day in the life of my new glasses, they met their demise.

My brother and I were playing war that morning and as my brother shot, I dove behind my hay bale wall. When I came back up, my brother screamed in horror.

The BB had hit my glasses and I was holding the parts in my hands, but that was not the worst of it. The broken lens from my glasses had cut my eyebrow and blood flowed down my face like a river.

We knew Mom was going to kill us, so we did what every kid in that circumstance would do. We walked right back home to Mom, walked straight up to her and as she hurried to find a wet rag to clean my face up, we lied.

We told her my 4-H steer swung his head up while I was pouring grain and hit me in the face. She believed us and I had to go get another pair of glasses.

Unfortunately, my BB gun story doesn't stop there. Three days later, we were at it again. Only this time my brother's gun was no longer working, so we were fighting over mine.

We were sitting in the pickup wrestling over my BB gun when someone accidentally pulled the trigger and low and behold, it was pumped and loaded.

That was the end to my Dad's pickup window. So, yet again, we bonded together and tried to think up some story to keep us out of trouble with Mom and Dad.

Dad had asked my brother and I to rope a cow that morning and get her calf sucking. We had some time to think while we roped the cow, tied her to the pickup, and pushed the calf up to her bag to suck.

"I got it!" My brother exclaimed and I listened intently to the big tale we were going to tell to get us out of a spanking we knew would kill us.

We marched up to Mom and Dad and told them of how my brother roped the cow and she swung around and her horn smashed into the window and broke it. It worked, but the funniest thing about that story is that we told them what really happened about ten years ago. We all laughed about it then.

I will never buy any kid a BB gun ever, no matter what. In fact, that is the one kind of gun I do not own and will never own.

I still remember the welts that the BBs left on my body and to this day, I still have a BB embedded in my leg. My husband has wanted me to remove it for years and I refuse to.

It is a reminder of my youth and how stupid youth can be. Moreover, I still hold it over my brother every now and then.

Well that is the black and white version of the shootout and now everyone knows the truth.

The Big Boom

I remember the summer I was eleven as being one of the best summers of my life. I had explored almost every inch of the mountains behind our house.

With exception to a forty-acre piece of land that was next to the mine. It contained a rather good-sized old fallen down shack. I decided it was the next leg of my exploring, so I saddled my horse and headed off. I reached the shack at about three in the afternoon. Being a kid and all, I decided to sleep at the shack since it was so late. A bunch of the neighbor's cows milled around outside the shack and kept waking me up.

All sorts of things run through an eleven-year-olds head when they hear a bump in the night. Bears, cougars, monsters, or people were the cause of those bumps. It was never just an ornery old cow trying to get that last bite of grass under the shack.

Come morning, I was glad to see the daylight. I quickly explored the shack and all it's contents to the fullest. I always made careful to never steal anything or disrupt anything in my adventures while on other people's property.

I never wanted to be told that I couldn't use the shack and it had great prospects of becoming a good place to camp.

However, I did explore it to the fullest. Every empty coffee can could hold a treasure. I examined the old glass bottles for any interesting ones for my collection, but as I remember, I never found one unbroken bottle in that shack.

The most exciting thing I found came in the form of two very small, long metal looking tubes. I found them wrapped up in some tissue and stored in an airtight glass jar above one of the rafters. I pulled them out and turned them over in my hands. I could not figure out what they were for the life of me, but they looked old.

I figured I would take them and show my parents. I had rode about a mile towards home when a thought hit me. "Blasting caps were small tubes. What if they were blasting caps and I was carrying them in my coat pocket."

My Uncle was a miner and he had once pulled some blasting caps out of the wall of my Grandfather's old cabin.

I stopped and carefully got off my horse at the edge of a cliff. I then pulled out the small tubes and chucked them over the edge of the cliff.

I heard the biggest boom that made both my horse and me jump. They were blasting caps and I had been carrying them in my pocket. I knew I had been lucky not to be killed by those tiny little tubes.

I didn't stop playing around the old shack or the mine but from then on if I didn't know what it was I never picked it up.

The Cougar Hunter

I had just turned sixteen and was coming home from basketball practice in my Dad's pickup. It was dark and snowing as I rounded the corner a mile from our house and saw a sight not many get to see. It all happened so fast, but I still see it ever so clearly in my mind.

My headlights illuminated the scene. A deer ran onto the road, which caused me to slam on the brakes, but before I could come to a stop a large brown object leaped from the edge of the road and onto the deer.

I knew what it was from the many times in my life I had seen one; it was a cougar. It grabbed the deer by the hips with both claws and clamped its teeth down into the deer's back.

I honked the horn and floored the gas pedal. The cougar paid me little attention as I bumped into it with the pickup. It pulled the helpless deer down on the road and leaped to its neck.

I jumped from the pickup and screamed. It was the first time in my life I did not have a gun. The deer fell to the ground and I realized there was little I could do for it.

Even if at this point if I could get the cougar off of it, the deer, most likely, was injured so badly it wouldn't live. The cougar turned its head and looked at me with its face covered in the deer's blood. I was about twenty steps in front of the pickup, and staring a hungry cougar in the face.

He turned away from the deer, crouched down, and stared at me as if seeing dessert. I slowly backed away towards the pickup. I felt my heart jump into my throat as I bumped against the pickup's bumper. The cougar took a half-crouched step towards me.

My big mouth had just gotten me in trouble again. I silently thanked God I had left the pickup door open. As I rounded the door, the cougar took about three fast steps towards me and then retreated back to the deer's carcass.

The feelings I felt were mixed. I felt relieved I was in the pickup and not cat food. However, I also felt a little irked. These were my mountains and I was at the top of the food chain, not the cougar.

I backed up the pickup and put it in first gear, then second, and then third as I steered right for the cougar. He jumped out of the way and I drove home to get my Dad and a gun.

When we returned the cougar was nowhere in sight, I guess he got the message. Dad and I pulled the deer off the road and went home to call a local cougar-hunter who had dogs.

The next morning arrived and with it the local cougar-hunter. As he stepped from the pickup and I saw the short stature, petite build of the guy who was supposed to be this great hunter. I couldn't help but laugh.

Somehow, I had expected a thick built tough looking guy with a no-nonsense demeanor. I had heard stories of him before, about him in fights and many other things.

He was dirty from head to toe and chewed Copenhagen like a child chews bubble gum. His hair was shoulder length and he looked a little worse for wear to say the least.

I was busy loading the pickup with hay bales to feed the cows, so I did not follow Dad over when he went to say, "Hi," and tell him what happened to me the night before. I could over hear them talking about cougar hunting and I have to admit the idea of cougar hunting has intrigued me to no end.

Soon the hunter and Dad made their way towards the pickup where I was busy stacking hay.

The man looked me up and down as if I might be his next chew of Copenhagen then with little effort he said, "Hello."

As Dad and him talked, I noticed he never took his eyes off me. It made me nervous. Maybe he had never seen anyone work before.

Then I heard my Dad tell him I was interested in shooting the cougar since I had a cougar tag. The man looked up at me and spat a chew of Copenhagen out of his mouth. I am guessing it was meant to hit the ground, but it never did. The gob of spit dripped off his chin and onto the third button of his shirt, where he let it stay. I almost puked. I might be a backwoods country bumpkin but he gave even hillbillies a bad rap.

"So you want to kill a cougar little lady? Yeah?" The man asked as again as he spat a pitiful stream of tobacco juice off his chin again. Only this time, I watched with horror as it made its way to the fifth button of his shirt.

"Yes I do." I answered.

"Well jump in my truck and we will go get you a cougar then, little lady." He said. I looked at the wreck he called a truck. From the outside, it was a driving heap of rusted metal.

I soon found that besides the two hound dogs that shared the seat with my rifle and me, there was another guy and two holes in the floor.

I was made to sit in the middle with the other guy driving and the cougar-hunter riding shotgun. But to top it all off, I had two dogs trying to lick my face and crawl over the top of me at the same time. It was a horrible ride. I clung to my riffle for all I was worth.

Once we stopped, a mile from the house, I was so glad to be out of the truck. I looked over the scene from the night before. I could tell the deer had been pulled another fifty-yards towards the tree line. Most likely, the cougar had come back during the night.

The dogs were quick to pick up a scent and the chase was on. We ran after them through the woods and up over the mountains. Down to the river and still farther. The dogs followed the cougar, the cougar-hunter followed the dogs, and I followed his smell.

When we finally reached the dogs the cougar hunter leashed them and handed one to me, saying, "Don't let him go, no matter what." So, we headed back to the truck. Halfway back he stopped and still holding his dog's leash leaned against a tree and stared at me.

"What?" I said.

"You know, you aren't very pretty." He said. "But I like my women that way."

I stared at him, dumbfounded.

"Do you pick up a lot of girls with that line?" I asked.

"If you don't mind. I would like to ask your father for permission to date you." At that point, I puked in my mouth and a sneeze could have knocked me over. I almost let go of the dog.

"My Dad doesn't allow me to date." I said as I continued up the trail.

"That is sure too bad, but he may make an exception for me. I will see." He said from somewhere behind me as I picked up the pace.

The ride to our place was miserable. He kept looking at me with a smile, which revealed the Copenhagen stuck between his tobacco stained teeth.

I was so happy to be back at our house I jumped from the pickup and headed for the house. I felt the need to shower or should I say scour.

I told Dad what happened and he laughed because it ends up cougar-hunter told Dad he would like to date me. My Dad, being the humorous guy that he is, decided to tell him that it was entirely up to me.

My Mom freaked, saying. "You will not date him!"

"Oh shucks Mom. You mean I can't date him and his Copenhagen chewing, barely off his chin spitting ways. Gosh you just ruined my whole life."

NOT!!!

Thistle Slope

It was fall and I was about to turn thirteen. It was getting awfully cold and according to most reports it was the last weekend of deer season so I decided I was going to go hunting. Grandpa happened to be heading up into the mountains to get some firewood and check on our cows that had spent the summer up there, so I asked if I could ride along.

After grabbing my old "tried and true" and a few bullets we were off. We drove leaving civilization behind. It was just Grandpa, me, and an old baby blue Jeep, who's brakes were getting a little tired but no more than the rest of the rig.

Grandpa said he was going to cut wood in the range corral draw so he would drive me to the back of Thistle Slope and from there it was only about three miles down to were he would be. The mountains were my home I knew them like the back of my hand so I had no worries about getting lost even though it would be dark in a couple hours. I had always heard Dad's stories of getting big mule deer over there so I figured it might be worth it.

Well about three-thirty Grandpa dropped me off, I quickly found a well used cow trail with fresh deer tracks. *Perfect!* I thought. My mind raced with plans of bringing home the biggest buck ever known to man. Suddenly I heard a crashing sound. Something was heading right for me. I knelt down, aiming my gun at the sound. BOOM...CRUNCH...BANG! Whatever it was, it was coming fast. With all of the buck brush, I knew then, if it was my trophy buck I would only have seconds to see it, shoot it, and jump for joy.

CRUNCH...THUMP...THUMP... It came into view not more than fifty-feet from me, a doe. She was gone as quick as she was seen. Shucks, no buck, oh well.

I got up. My heart racing a little and my eyes searching the slopes for her man. Suddenly, a blur raced by me not more than ten- feet away. Wow, a spike! I figured I must have been in the express lane or something. Again, he was gone and all that was left was me sitting dumbfounded on the trail staring after him. Maybe deer season had changed to hunter season. Maybe the deer applied for tags and hunted us. Well he must have had the same feelings about me as I had for him, not big enough.

My heart still racing and darkness closing in I figured I had better keep moving. There was an apple tree I knew about a couple hundred yards farther and it always had good apples. Coming over a small rise I found I wasn't the only one who knew it was the best tree on the hillside for about thirty cows stood huddled around the base.

I walked over. The cows didn't move much and they seemed happy to see me. After climbing the tree and selecting a couple of the best looking apples and taking a bite out of a couple more I climbed down thanking the cows for their hospitality and heading off across the slope towards the draw. One of the cows seemed more eager to follow me than to stay with her friends, she followed about a hundred yards behind.

I threw a rock at her hoping she would leave me alone to hunt in peace, no luck she didn't even seem bothered. With her head to the ground she just kept on following me. I was not going to see any deer with a cow following behind me. It was going to be like trying to fit through a cat hole with a big butt, it's just not going to happen.

Finally, after ducking behind a tree in the draw, she turned around, obviously losing interest in me. After I knew she was gone, I climbed back out of the draw and followed the trail out onto the slope again.

It was about five o'clock now and in about an hour I knew it would be dark so I figured if there were any deer hiding in the draw they should be moving by now. So I found an old tree whose roots were sticking crudely out of the ground. I nestled in between two huge roots that were about chest high when I sat. I had found the perfect place to sit and watch the last two hundred yards of Thistle Slope before the hillside turned into a thick ravine and I was only about a mile from where grandpa was cutting wood.

I slipped off my vest and coat and draped them over my legs. After fidgeting around and getting comfortable, I was finally able to sit quietly enough to hear something coming up behind the tree, that damned cow! Setting my gun down I figured I was going to give her the scare of her life. I was going to jump around the tree on my hands and knees and yell boo at her, I chuckled to myself I knew I would ruin my hunt but this cow was driving me nuts, it was about time someone taught her a lesson.

"Boo!" I yelled as I bounded over the root to my right and landed on my hands and knees, Oh shoot! my cow didn't look so much like a cow anymore. Hunched down not more than two feet away from my face were the prettiest green eyes I have ever seen; almost hypnotizing. I froze, fear hung in the air. I knew that in about two seconds my life would be over. A cougar, natures most unforgiving animal, stared into my eyes. A snarl left his mouth, his teeth looked so clean and white in the dusk, I dropped my eyes away from his, the whoosh of wind swept past my face as his paw barely missed my cheek.

I looked at the earth below my hands knowing soon it would be my blood that covered it. What was he waiting for why wasn't he eating me, not that I was eager or anything. I slowly raised my eyes. What! He was gone. I guess he thought I wasn't big enough either, this small thing was getting real discouraging. I reached slowly back around the tree and grabbed my gun. Where were you when I needed you?

I grabbed my vest and coat and stood shaking for a moment. Oh shoot, it's getting dark and he might change his mind. I jacked a bullet into the chamber and started down the hill. Slowly my walk got quicker until I was running heedlessly down the slope.

That's when I heard footsteps off to my right, he was following me. I turned but lost my footing and tumbled head over heels with my loaded gun down a steep incline. I could have sworn I caught a glimpse of those pearly whites laughing at me. But when the world stopped spinning and I shook the dizzies away I was alone on the floor of the ravine. What a quick way to get down, I had to only be a couple hundred yards from the road, then a few more hundred yards till I found Grandpa.

Oh shoot! My gun where is my gun it was darker in the ravine and I felt the ground around me, frantically searching. My hands touched the cold steel of the barrel. Oh, thank God. I got up and looked around he was out there somewhere I knew that much and started towards the road.

I felt safer after reaching the road, and started to move towards the sound of the chainsaw. I had enough deer hunting for one day. As I rounded the corner, I realized I had to compose myself a little but I was shaking so hard what was the use.

"Grandpa, we need to go now," I said as calmly as I could muster.

"Go? Why, did you get something"

"No, but I think I pissed off a big cat Grandpa a really big cat" I emphasized with my arms

"A big cat?" he asked

"Yeah Grandpa, big cat... Grrrr, chased me, fall down hill, aaaaaaaaaaaaaa, need to go home now, and change shorts."

I could tell that Grandpa didn't quite get what I was trying to explain, it just wouldn't come out right. I threw all of his tools into the Jeep, only for him to unload some of them and go back to work. Then, I proceeded to load them up again trying to move the process of getting the heck off the mountain up.

"Okay," he said, "let's get the last of this firewood loaded then we'll go back for supper."

I threw firewood the size of a truck into the back of the Jeep and everything else again. For the third time, after looking around a little more, finally getting in and were off.

Back at the house I was able to explain a little better after some of my color came back and I had some hot cocoa, which Grandpa laced with a little Black Velvet while everyones heads were turned.

Nowadays, looking back, all I remember about telling the story to my family that day was that my mother said that I need to learn to tell my stories without cussing, She'd be glad to know that I reduced this story down from what it was the first time I told it.

Cowboys and Indians

I was eleven years old and into everything, I could do with my horse. My brother and I would play Cowboys and Indians on a regular basis.

On such a day I decided to jump on Bee to get away from my brother. Up I climbed, bareback with bailing twine for a bridle and away I ran.

I had a play gun stuffed into the waistband of my jeans. Every now and then, I would turn and fire it at my brother.

As I remember it, we had played for hours until my mother called us to come home for supper. I ran my horse down the county road and turned up towards the barn when I heard my brother yell, "Bang! You're dead!"

I let go of the bailing twine and flung myself off the side of my horse as I had done about a hundred times that day.

I hit the soft sand and Bee came to an abrupt halt. I lay in the sand gripping at my chest until my brother walked from behind some bushes with his pistol in hand.

As he neared, I rolled over, pulling my own pistol from my waistband and shot him. He fell back and his gun went flying.

I stood still gripping my make believe bullet hole and made my way to where he lay unmoving. As I neared, I heard him moan. I pulled my pistol up to finish him off when he kicked my feet out from underneath me.

This time I fell for real and as I lay on the ground, he attacked me with a brotherly array of punches. I kicked him in the stomach and stood up throwing sand in his face.

My brother cursed and leaped across the road to tackle me again. I bit his arm and he screamed out in pain, punched me in the arm, and took off running.

I jumped up on my horse and headed straight for him. He dodged out of the way and pulled me off my horse as we ran by.

We wrestled and fought on the ground for a few moments before he took off running cross-country heading for home. I got up and shook the sand out of places I would rather not discuss.

That's about when I saw that a small car was parked at the base of the driveway. A lady rolled her window down and the look on her face was pure concern.

"We saw almost the whole thing. Are you Okay?" She asked.

"Yeah."

"Do you know who he was? We could call the cops." She said.

"Naw, it happens all the time." I said as I bent and picked up my gun off the ground and stuffed it back in my waistband. "I'll get him next time."

The lady screamed and yelled at her husband. "Go! Go! Go! She has a gun!"

I did not have enough time to tell her it was a fake gun. However, I do remember the car and the fact that it had Canadian license plates.

I am sure that they were thinking they had just driven back in time to the days of the old west.

Fun and Games

I am sure most of you have heard the saying, "It is all fun and games until someone gets hurt." Well it is, or, in my case, it is all fun and games until someone forgets about where you are.

My older brother and I used to raise steers for 4-H every year since we were eight. Every morning after feeding the main herd of cows and before school we had to feed our 4-H steers. Off we would go, across the county road, and up a road to where our feedlot was. We would feed our steers and then play for a few minutes if time allowed and sometimes when time didn't allow.

On one such morning, when I was eleven, we decided to play Cowboys and Indians and on that particular morning, I was the Cowboy. Which was unusual because usually I was the Indian and he was the Cowboy and he would say Cowboys had guns and Indians only had bows and arrows.

"Bang! You're dead."

We had this rule that if you were shot you had to count to twenty before getting up and fighting back. We also had to count out loud. So every time I hit twenty. "Bang!" I was dead again. I would count and then "Bang!" I was killed again. I would get mad and say, "I wasn't playing." Then my brother would allow me to get up and find some cover before he shot me again.

Well, like I said, on that morning I got to be the Cowboy so I pulled out my imaginary gun and before I could say bang he grabbed my hands and drug me to the old apple tree.

"Indians used to burn Cowboys." He said. I fought as my four-year-older brother tied my hands behind my back and around the apple tree.

"Let me go!" I yelled. "I am going to tell Mom." I warned.

About that time, my Mom yelled for us to come. My brother took off running for home and left me there.

I knew he was going to tell Mom that I took off and had told him "I was not going to school," I had done that before. I also knew Mom had to be at work on time.

I worked at the ropes that bound my hands but they wouldn't budge. I yelled, but with my cold it was no use, I could barely hear myself.

I listened as my Mom yelled for me to get my butt to the house or she was leaving without me. Then in horror I heard her car start up and head towards school.

I worked all day trying to get my wrist unbound from those darn ropes until finally about one-thirty, my hero, my Grandfather showed up and found me. It wasn't the first time he had rescued me from one of my brother's attempts of torturing me.

He once found me hanging from the rafters of the grainery where my brother had fastened a noose and gave me a coffee can to stand on. It was one of those Wild West games we played.

Another time he found me on top of one of the haystacks where, when I climbed onto it, my brother took the ladder away.

"You know." He said as he untied my hands. "You two are going to have to find something else to play, or else one of these times I might not find you in time to save you."

Grandpa was always famous for one quote he used to say. Mostly when I tormented one of the cats but he used to say it about a lot of things.

"If you wreck it, you can't fix it." He used to say that to my brother about me. "If you wreck her, you can't fix her."

To which my brother would reply. "Who'd want to fix her?" You have got to love older brothers.

It was all fun and games.

Future Roper

The problem with being a younger sister is that a bigger brother means that his friends are all that size too. It was a problem I learned to deal with.

Three older boys have ganged up on me up with BB guns playing war. I have had apples thrown at me by three older boys after kicking one of them in the 'yoo hoos' for pushing me down in the cow poop. They tied my cousin and I up to a tree one time and left us while they went for cake and ice cream. I froze all winter because one of his friends decided to put his big butt through our bedroom window.

However, the most memorable stories came around the time that my brother and one of his best friends decided they were going to grow up to be ropers. I knew when they first started talking about it that the combination of them with ropes and horses, it was a bad idea. I was right.

First, it was just them asking me to run so that they could practice roping. In the beginning, I did because they never caught me. Pretty soon, however, I stopped participating because they got so they could actually catch me every once in a while. The main problem there was that they weren't happy with just catching me.

If they would have just caught me and then turned me loose it wasn't so bad. But, NO! They had to rope me and then try to drag me like they were on horses and their horses wouldn't stop.

Eventually, I refused to run for them, and while they were outside practicing, I refused to leave the house. Pretty soon, they started coming in after me while Mom and Dad were at work and dragging me outside. I couldn't stand still or they would rope me.

Many times, I would run over the hill and keep on going until I heard Mom or Dad's pickups pull up and then I would come out of hiding.

However, sometimes they would hold onto me while the other one roped me. I told Grandpa what they were doing to me and he got after them. He also told me that I should just get on my old horse and go explore the mountains to keep away from them until Mom and Dad came home.

It was on such a day that this story really starts. I had bridled my horses and jumped on her from a nearby fence rail. Then we headed through the pasture and up to the road towards the mountains. At the base of the road, you have to go through a gate in order to go higher and sitting in the road in the middle of the gate was my brother and his friend with their ropes.

I told them to leave me alone. Then I kicked my horse into a gallop and headed straight towards them. My brother grabbed at the bridle while his friend roped me. I felt the rope tighten around my neck and I hung on for all I could. My brother let go of the horse's bridle and off she took and off the back of my horse, I flew. I hit with a thud and it took the wind out of me.

I got up and loosened the rope from around my neck. My neck hurt and I could tell I was most likely rope burned.

"Mom is going to kill you two!" I yelled.

"Please don't tell her." My brother begged. I hit him and walked off to retrieve my horse.

"I will feed your 4-H steer for the next three days." My brother said.

I knew I was in a bargaining position. So I asked for the one thing I had always wanted the most from my brother and his friends.

"If you two promise to stop picking on me, I won't tell Mom."

"For a week?" My brother bargained.

I knew that was better than nothing so I agreed.

My neck was red and rope burned. It looked like someone had tried to hang me, but I kept my part of the deal and didn't tell Mom or anyone else.

Monday morning came and at school, I just tied a red handkerchief around my neck to hide the raw and icky rope burn. I got a lot of cowboy jokes aimed at me that day. However, nobody seemed to laugh when gym class came and I was told to take off the handkerchief.

I said to my gym teacher, "No." Then as everyone stood around and listened, the teacher reached up, untied it, and yanked it off.

Well if you have ever had a rope burn or a burn of any kind you know that they weep fluid. When that teacher pulled the handkerchief off I didn't realize that some of that goo had stuck to the handkerchief. With the removal of the handkerchief went the scab that had formed throughout the day on that rope burn. Blood poured from the line across my neck.

The horror on the teacher's face and the other kid's faces was shocking.

"What happened to you?" The teacher screamed as she grabbed a towel and pressed it to my throat and rushed me down to the nurse's station.

"My brother roped me off my horse." I confessed.

"He what?" The teacher asked.

"He roped me off my horse." I said again.

"He could have killed you." The teacher said and the nurse agreed with a nod.

"Well, he is going to be a roper when he grows up." I said as if that explained it all.

You know what the horrible part of this story is? My brother never became a roper, even after all that.

Three Miles To Go

Growing up I often heard my elders talking, they would say, "The hardest times is the grease that lubes the wheel of life." I am not sure about that grease stuff but I hit an awful hard time in my life when I was about twenty-three.

My husband and I were so happy, we had just got engaged. That wasn't what made it my hardest time by any means. Let me state, in case he reads this, that it is just a time line for the story.

My father had called that morning about five-thirty, "That old roan cow and her calf have jumped the fence and are in with the neighbors cows. My horse is too close to foaling to ride. Would you come chase her in for me?" He exclaimed.

"Of course I will." I saddled my gelding, Colt, and drove the two hours back home to get old roan and her calf out of the neighbors herd. I found a note on the door telling me him and Mom went to Colville to see about some parts for the tractor and to just chase her back into the top pasture. She shouldn't give me any problems.

I tightened my cinch, grabbed my gun and climbed aboard. Colt took to the mountains like he had been born in them, he wanted to run up but I knew we might have a long ride ahead so I kept him reined in. We rode for about two hours looking and searching for the spot where the cows had crossed. Finally, I found where the fence was down. I fixed it and opening the gate so later I could bring her through. Now, we were ready to find her.

We seemed to be climbing and descending mountains for miles. We rode until we could see darkness drawing near. We were riding down a thick ravine when I heard something move up ahead. Circling around behind it I realized it was a small group of cows. I scanned the herd for any sign of a roan cow. There she was, with her calf sucking, standing under an old pine tree.

I could tell the cows were spooky, so I climbed the hill until I could move to the right of the herd and then if they got frightened they would run straight down the mountain. We stood atop an eighty-some degree sloped hillside that looked like a monster. I urged Colt off of it, when suddenly the cows took off. I reacted without realizing my horse was already running as fast as he could straight down this incline.

Everything happened so quickly. I felt the earth give way under his pounding feet. He sped up, frightened, and I hung on for all I was worth. I felt his front end quake and fall, his hind quarters were going over my head. The saddle was on top of me and then I was being flung over his head as we did another summersault. Then he came down again on top of me. I knew in the back of my mind that I had to get away from him or I was going to die right here on the mountain I called home.

After another flip I was sent flying to the right and him to the left. I lay on the ground with my face in the dirt trying to figure out if I was dead or alive. Slowly, I got to my feet with my head spinning, and I fell down again. If equilibrium was something everybody had, I should have asked for seconds. I rested my head on my knees until I found a little more. Colt, where was he?

I looked around. My eyes came to rest on the still body of my gelding. I stumbled towards him while wiping the blood out of my eye. Oh, God I begged, don't let him be dead or injured so badly that I had to put him down right here and now. I had seen a horse put down once before and I prayed I would never have to put one down myself.

He wasn't moving but his eyes followed me as I came near. He tried to stand but fell back down. I quickly checked his legs for breaks, none, his back I checked it frantically...nothing. Sitting back on my heels, I realized maybe he was as mixed up as I was. Again, he tried to get up. That is when I saw one of his reins had wrapped around his leg and he couldn't get up. After relieving him of the tangled rein I helped him get to his feet, he was pretty banged up, but he would live.

So with my face cut to shreds and bleeding something fierce all over my new white t-shirt, and Colt barely able to walk we managed to limp out the three miles to my parent's place. That was the longest three miles of my life and probably Colt's too.

It was pitch dark by the time we reached my parent's house, no one was home yet. I still had to drive the two hours back home so I could get my gelding to the vet first thing in the morning. My face was a mess, mostly little scratches except for one. So I quickly unsaddled and loaded Colt. I made him comfy with some straw for bedding, and some hay to munch.

I thought about stopping at the hospital and having them stitch up my face, but it would take them too long and who knows, they might say I had a concussion or something. There was no way I was going to take the chance of having to spend the night in town. I grabbed a sewing needle and some cow sutchers and went to work on my face, it may not have been pretty but it worked.

With my face stitched and my horse comfy we headed home. My face bled something terrible on the way home and the stitches hurt worst than if the cut was open. I cut open the stitches while on the ferry boat and just left it open.

It was almost midnight by the time I reached home. I figured everybody would have gone to bed. No, low and behold, my father-in-law had waited up to make sure I made it home alright. Any other night I would have been grateful but not with me looking like the living dead. I knew I looked horrible.

I inched into the house after settling Colt down in the barn. By the look on his face, you would have thought the whole Halloween cosmetics factory had blown up all around me. If I would have looked as bad as they made it out to be, Colt should have put me down up on that hill.

Well the vet told me Colt had "stress foundered" but he would recover in a couple of months. I must have stopped by a newspaper office on the way home, because in the next couple of weeks I heard some pretty amazing stories about what happened up on that mountain. I was pretty impressed with my quick wit and fast guns in a couple of the stories. And they seem to keep growing longer and longer with each new version.

But here is the real story, and if by some strange coincidence you should here one of the longer ones do me a small favor. If it's a good one just sit back and listen, no use changing what doesn 't need to be changed.

I doubt if it would be a smaller story you might hear, but in that case, feel free to add what you see fit. But whatever the story, you have now heard the true "Three Mile Story."

The Escape

I was eleven-years-old and was into everything. Trouble was my first, middle, and last name according to anybody you asked.

A friend of mine and I decided to skip the last two days of school and disappear for a few weeks up into the mountains. We saddled the horses, grabbed some food, and took off. I knew of an old mine shack that was not used anymore ,so we decided to stay there for a few nights.

I remember everything about that night as clearly as if it had happened yesterday. We got to the shack at about ten-thirty at night. We noticed there was a light on inside, you could see it through the window. I knew nobody lived there and the old mine had been shut down for some years. The land was up for sale but nobody had bought it because of the cyanide pond.

So we crept around to the draw and tied our horses up. Curiosity had won and we had to see who was in that shack. I grabbed my twenty-two off the saddle and loaded it; just in case bad guys jumped out and started firing at us like in all the John Wayne movies.

As we snuck up towards the cabin we could hear voices inside but couldn't make out a word they were saying. My friend was freaking out and I had to hush her more than once. I tried to get her to go back to the horses and wait for me, but she was convinced that they were killers and they were going to kill me and then she would never be able to find her way home. Her confidence in my shooting was flattering to say the least.

My silent sneaking was being ruined by her trying to drag me back to the horses. I finally allowed her to usher me back to where the horses were tied.

"You can't go up there, they will kill you!" she yelled. I clasped my hand over her mouth. Gosh almighty, I was going to kill her if she didn't stop yelling.

I finally convinced her to sit on top of Bee. I told her, "If anything happens to me kick Bee and she would find her way home." That was one thing Bee could do with her eyes shut.

So with that all settled, I snuck back up to the window. The voices inside were yelling at each other in a rather harsh manner. The windows needed to be cleaned and were so grimy I couldn't make out anything that was going on inside.

They talked about some money that they obviously had a quarrel over. They spoke about sneaking stuff across the border. They discussed how to do it better next time. I heard three different voices, they all sounded male and figured they were drug runners.

I realized they probably wouldn't be very happy if they knew a kid was hearing all their plans so I snuck back to where my friend was waiting. I couldn't find her or the horses. I was worried she might have gotten caught when I wasn't paying attention. So back to the shack I snuck. No, they were still deep in conversation; besides, I would have heard her scream.

That was when I said the first cuss word I ever remember saying. She took off and left me, probably hell bent for my house. It was so dark there was no way I was going to be able to find her and the horses even if I took off running as fast as I could, and it was quite a distance to the road where we came in on.

I knew the shack stealers had to have a mode of transportation. I just had to find it. I snuck around the shack until I found it two four-wheelers. I started ripping wires and anything else that was loose out of one of them then I pushed the other one as far as I could away from the shack. I had never ridden a four wheeler and wasn't sure I could even start it.

I jumped on and managed to get the starting technique right on the third try. I hit every button and switch I could find and finally got it moving forward. I kept hitting the shifter and it just kept going faster and faster, which was fine by me.

I never looked back until I got to the old road. I hid the four wheeler in a bunch of brush and took off running for home. It was still about four miles, but I didn't care. I don't think I slowed down the whole way home. I am pretty sure anyone would say that adrenalin was my main drive. That and the fact that my friend had probably already told my parents some horrific story and the police were probably headed this way.

When I got to the house, she was already there, wailing away and telling my parents I was probably killed by now. They couldn't get her to calm down enough to understand her. I just told them we were playing cowboys and indians and she got scared and took off.

We laugh about it now, but at the time, I could have killed her myself..

I never heard any reports of a missing four-wheeler, nor did I ever tell my parents about it either. My great escape from the shack stealers.

Roll Over

I was thirteen and that was the first problem. I had a black lab slash mutt and that was the second problem. However, the biggest problem behind this story was a deer. That's right, a deer, a small brown colored, hundred and some odd pound deer.

It was ten thirty at night and snowing as hard as I could remember. We had a cow calving down below our house and Dad had asked me to take the pickup and to go check on her.

I jumped at the chance even though I was not real new to driving. I had already been driving all over the ranch for a couple of years. As I left the house, Mom said, "If you're going down the county road put on your seat belt."

As I put the pickup in first gear, I latched the seatbelt, shifted the four-wheel drive into high, and drove out of the driveway. I had to go down the county road to where I could find the cow.

When I got to her, I parked the pickup on the side of the road and turned the spotlight on her. I saw the calf was already up and trying to suck.

I knew because of the narrow road I was going to have to go down the road to where there was wide spot and turn around.

My dog, Gabby, followed as I drove in second gear down the road. Once I was turned around, I unsnapped my seatbelt, stopped the pickup, and flipped the radio on. I didn't recognize the song the station was playing, but it was country. I put the pickup in gear and started home. After I shifted into second gear, I held it at about fifteen to twenty miles per hour.

Suddenly out of nowhere a deer jumped in front of me with my dog Gabby right on it's heels. I swerved ever so slightly to miss my dog and felt pure panic as the edge of the bank gave way to the weight of the pickup.

I remember the first rollover in slow motion. I went up, hit my head against the ceiling, then came down, and landed on the floor where I hit the radio button on the way down.

The station changed from country to a religious station. The man on the radio was deep in a sermon saying, "God has given and God shall taketh away." I will never forget that line ever in my whole life.

As the pickup rolled again, my Dad's rifle hit me in the head as it flew from the gun rack in the back window. The hill was only about thirty to forty feet but the pickup rolled three times coming to rest upright on it's tires.

Everything was dark. I was stunned and couldn't move. I thought I was dead and buried and somehow my parents had found the most uncomfortable coffin they could buy. I noticed there was something hard poking me in the back.

I slowly moved my hand and realized I was cold. "Well that can't be." I said. I thought for sure after I died I would be hot. Very Hot.

Slowly I reached up and touched my face. Something was wrong! I couldn't feel my face! I panicked and sat straight up. My coat fell off of my face.

I looked at it and laughed. That is, until I remembered what happened. "Dad is going to kill me."

I looked out the window and saw the lights were still on. One pointed straight out and the other pointed straight up. I got out of the pickup and I could see the damage, even in the dark.

I knew I was dead. I walked the mile back to the house and was instantly greeted by Mom and the words I was dreading, "Dawn where is the pickup?"

"In the neighbor's field." I replied. "I rolled it." Mom and I went down to get Dad's gun and that's when I first wished I hadn't lived through the rollover.

We found his gun under the pickup, broken in two. I remember asking my Mom if it would still shoot. She said, "Yes, but you can't aim it."

I told her she wouldn't have to aim. I just wanted her to shoot me. I didn't want to tell my Dad his gun was broken. The pickup he didn't yell about, but the gun he did.

In the light of the following day, we got a good look at the pickup when they got it back to the house. In the drivers side seat was a hunk of metal from the door that had flew off and stuck in the seat about three inches.

That was the first time I didn't listen to my Mom that I didn't get in trouble.

The Horses

Horse Thief

Spring of my seventeenth year Mom and Dad thought it was time for me to get off my mountain and go out into the world. It was to be my first time off the ranch and I was, to say the least, scared out of my mind.

So after searching for about a month for the perfect summer job I submitted an application to a dude ranch that was looking for wranglers. I heard shortly back from them saying I was hired and would I come as soon as possible. So I kissed Gadjet goodbye and said "farewell" to my mountain for the summer. Oh, how I was going to miss it, but I knew that I was going to find adventure in the outside world.

I cried the whole three hours to the big city as I drove myself to my Aunt's house I was to spend the night with her and catch a train the next morning at

1:00 A.M. So carrying my saddle and a small bag I boarded the 1:00 A.M. train to Montana. I had barely ever been out of my home town let alone out of the state. The stewardess told me I was going to have about a twelve hour trip and that I should make myself comfortable.

From the train windows, I watched the countryside go by and I watched the strange looking people bustle around the train. I barely spoke to anyone and didn't want to look anyone in the eyes. I watch the news, I know what people do, they kill people for looking at them cross-eyed. I wasn't back home on my mountain any longer I had to watch who I talked to. My aunt told me not to speak or associate with anyone on the train.

Finally, we were there. The train depot was scary, there were people everywhere. Oh, what was I thinking leaving home. I wanted to sit down in a corner and cry, thank goodness a man came forward and introduced himself as a wrangler at the ranch. We got into his truck and took a two hour drive up some road to some little tiny stable that barely held twelve horses.

After spending the day there learning all their ways, I was picked up by two girls in a little tiny sports car who didn't talk to me and drove another three hours in the opposite direction to an even littler stable. It had a corral with about two feet of mud in it and twenty some of the most miserable looking horses you ever did see. They were covered in mud. If they dared to roll after a ride they would look like mud pies in the morning.

I was disgusted to say the least. I immediately called home and told my parents of the horrible state of their animals, my mother said to try to stick it out. Some people don't love their animals the way you do she assured me. I was disgusted with the treatment of the animals, but I vowed to stick it out.

Pay was to be seven hundred a month. We were to work six days a week with one day off, from three in the morning till dark.

The next morning, after a great breakfast, we headed out to the horse corrals to saddle the horses. All the horses were saddled but one, a large sorrel gelding who I was told fell and hurt his back and now he bucks everybody off. If I was a horse, I would buck all of them off too.

We had an instant kinship. I would sneak grain and carrots out to him when no one was watching, usually after everyone was asleep or before they woke up.

The days seemed to drift into weeks, I hated it. I still hadn't had a day off and the other wranglers laughed at me when I had no clue what some disgusting thing was. However, the sorrel and I had become best of friends. I was able to massage the disc in his back into place and in the darkness of the night I would brush him and ride him on short rides, he never once offered to buck.

A month had passed and everybody else had gotten paid but me and I still had no days off on the calendar. So I went to talk to the boss he said he didn't have time to talk to me and that I would be paid soon. Four more days came and went, still no pay, still no days off. I started to ride the sorrel on the rides with guests, then the day came that my outside adventure began.

We were up at base and I had left the sorrel with my saddle on him, tied to the rail and went to the bathroom. When I came out, one of the other wranglers, who didn't seem to care for me very much, was getting a guest mounted on him.

We all had our assigned horses and the sorrel was mine. I asked why she had put anyone, let alone a three hundred pound man, on my horse. She said the boss wanted to start using him for guests again. However, as the man came astride the sorrel, I believe he realized that it was not me and took to bucking. He bucked right over the fence throwing his rider and continued down through the draw.

I started after him on foot when the boss yelled for me to leave him alone. "Hell I will," I said, My saddle is on him and he was just scared." Boss said he would bring back my saddle because he was going to go put that horse down once and for all.

I begged him to sell him to me. I said he could keep my pay for the month and we would call it even.

He laughed, "I am not paying you for the first month, it's just a trial period and it's over. I want you gone tomorrow."

I was so mad I ran at his horse he was riding and pulled the bridle over it's ears and out of his mouth. Then I took off down the draw towards the sorrel.

I found him and climbed aboard we flew out of there like the devil was on our heels. Well the devil might not have been, but the police were. Cop cars lined the road looking for me. I ran for about two-miles, then I stopped to give the sorrel a break, I could hear the sirens coming down the road. If I was back home they would never have caught me.

I didn't know the area and I seemed to be running headlong into the police everywhere I turned. I panicked and tried to make it through the park gates. Nets seemed to come out of thin air, I was caught. I kicked and screamed I tried to explain to the police, but I was escorted out of Montana and the sorrel was sent to the canner.

I called every canner I could, sending pictures of the sorrel, but alas I never heard back.

To this day, I still carry a photo of him and hope I will see him walk through the door at some horse sale. I hold a small hope that somebody saved him. He was a truly kindred spirit and will always hold a piece of my heart.

We almost made it, and you know to this day I have only told few people what actually happened in Montana all those many years ago.

The Bay Gelding

About seven years ago, I bought a big bay gelding who was supposed to have had thirty days riding and be very gentle. It was about an hour drive each way to go pick him up. I put him in a corral and figured I would let him calm down a bit as he was bouncing off the corral right and left.

The next morning I got up early and drove to the barn to feed and water him. I ran a hose into his pen and threw some hay over the fence. I figured I would be nice and give him a scoop of oats. I grabbed a small bucket and after placing two scoops in it and retrieving a pan I opened the gate and stepped in.

I had no more stepped in and turned to close the gate when a hoof struck me on the shoulder. I fell and turned to see the bay gelding rearing above me for another strike. I crawled to the panel and felt him come down on my legs with his hooves. I tried to pull myself under the panel when he struck me along side the head with a hoof Again. My world went black for a moment and I figured this is where I was going to die.

He kept pawing me and biting me until I was able to get under the fence, he stood on the other side still trying to bite me through the panel. I laid on the ground not knowing what to do or why he was doing this to me.

I crawled into the pickup and couldn't remember how to start it. I made my way back home, but to this day I am not sure how as I do not remember the drive. I called my husband and relayed what had happened. Nobody could believe it; not the lady who sold me the horse or anyone else.

We figured maybe it was a fluke and he was just scared. We left him alone for a few days and then sent him to a trainer. After describing what happened the trainer agreed to see if it was the horse's attitude or if I had just scared him.

It took the trainer just minutes to almost get killed and give us his opinion of the bay gelding.

I called other trainers and asked them what to do. One stated that he would like to give him a try, so I invited him down to try to do something with the bay gelding.

It took him six seconds to get back out of the corral after a near fatal attempt on his life. He looked at me and said very bluntly. "The bay gelding needs to go to the slaughter yards before he killed someone."

I was horrified, but I did not want to give up on the bay. I fed and cared for him for three months but never dared step inside the pen with him.

I called trainers upon trainers who refused to touch him or even look at him. I decided I would do it myself. For the next three more months I tried to make him my friend over the fence.

I brought him treats and grain. Slowly I got so that I could pet his nose without him trying to bite me or strike at me. I knew that if this gelding had thirty days of riding then he must have let someone get near him so I tried everything I could think of to make him my friend.

Exactly seven months after I first brought him home I decided to try to walk in to pet him again. I opened the gate slowly and was pleased when he turned and looked at me taking one slow step in my direction.

I stepped inside never taking my eyes off of the bay gelding. He took another easy step towards me. I held still and waited as he stepped nearer. I was sure I had made him my friend when he stepped up and sniffed my face.

I was still afraid to move. He sniffed my hand and then my world went black. A hoof struck my collarbone and another came crushing down on my forehead. I fell under him and he continued to stomp and walk over the top of me.

I managed, yet again, to crawl under the fence and escape his flying hooves and teeth. Again, I found myself unable to start the pickup and go the few miles home. This time I crawled or walked.

I called my husband and had to tell him that the horse beat me up again. He said no more and I agreed. The next day I drove the bay gelding to the local sale yard.

I wrote on his sale slip with deep regret, "Slaughter Only." I didn't want anyone else to buy him and get hurt.

I sat in the audience and watched as the bay gelding charged into the arena and just about took a chunk out of the arm of one of the arena men.

They started the bidding at fifty-dollars. I noticed a lady in the front row was bidding and the auctioneer was taking her bids.

When the bidding was done the auctioneer said, "Sold, at three hundred dollars." and then said the ladies name. I knew she had a bunch of kids and was operating an animal rescue.

I stood up. "No! Sell him again!" I said, "This horse is for slaughter only." The lady spat and sputtered in the front row.

"I bought him. You said, 'sold,' he is mine." She yelled.

"This horse is for slaughter only." I said again. "Do you see my face and here look at this." I pulled my collar down so she could see that my neck and shoulder were black from the bruising from the bay gelding.

"He did this to me twice. He isn't going to hurt anyone else." I sat down and told the auctioneer to resell him.

"I want that horse." The lady stammered again.

"Lady you have children. Why would you want this horse on your place? He could kill one of them!" I asked.

"He was just misunderstood." She whimpered.

"Lady, he has done this twice to me and almost killed two trainers. He is going to the soap factory and I am going to buy the first bar of soap from him and take a bath."

The auction barn broke into a round of laughs and I watched as the lady obviously mad stand up.

"I bought that horse. I want that horse." She yelled.

About that time, that damned bay gelding flung both hind feet out and kicked the arena man square in both knees.

As he hit the ground, the bay swung around and charged with teeth bared. The poor man didn't have a chance. The bay grabbed him by the shoulder and swung him over the fence.

The man stood and limped up to the lady in the front row.

He looked right at her and smiled up at me.

"I get the second bar of soap."

My Friend

I remember really meeting her for the first time when I was three-years-old even though she had been around the ranch and my grandpa rode her weekly. When my grandfather put me on her and gave me the reins and turned me loose, she did everything I had asked and I instantly became a horse lover forever in those few minutes that I rode her.

Her name was Bee. She was a big nine-year-old chestnut mare. She wasn't very fast at high speeds, but nothing unsettled her. From that day on when I went to grandpa's I would beg to ride Bee and he would, of course, give in and let me ride her in the yard.

For some reason, if he said I couldn't ride her one day I would be satisfied to just go sit by the gate of her pasture and talk to her. I was never allowed to go in without him of course.

When I was six I started school. I remember drawing pictures of Bee and making up stories in creative writing of Bee and I fighting dragons in some far off lands or getting that one cow off the mountain that no one else could get.

I got into my very first fist-fight in school when a kid made fun of a photo of Bee and I chasing cows. He said she looked fat. I jumped over two desks and one chair to sock him in the jaw.

By the time I turned ten we had moved twice; once to an old house in town until my parents set up the ranch house for us to move into. That meant I was within walking distance of Bee. My mother would say I took every available opportunity to abuse the situation. By this time I was riding Bee alone down to the river and up to the new ranch while my parents worked on the house.

The second move was up to the ranch where I was allowed to move Bee up with me so that every morning when I fed my 4-H steer I could see or ride her. Every afternoon after school I would jump on her bareback and we would take off to explore the mountains surrounding the ranch.

During the summer months we would take off into the mountains for weeks at a time, just Bee and I. We explored every nook and cavern within a five mile radius.

Some mornings, when I had to ride to my grandfather's to catch the bus I would detour to the river and stay there all day until I would see the school bus go by and then I would climb aboard Bee and back home, we would go.

When I was ten years old my brother, who was four years older, had just got his first motorbike. My Dad had received a phone call one morning that my grandfather's big Hereford bull had come down the mountain next to our place and had ended up in our neighbor's yard.

The neighbor called and said he was bleeding pretty bad, so my brother and his best friend hoped on their bikes and headed after him. I asked Dad if I could go on Bee and follow along in search of the bull. He said that my brother and his friend on their bikes would find him and I would most likely just be in the way.

I was pretty upset that I couldn't go. Mom came over to the horse corral, found me, and told me to saddle up and go, but to stay out of the way. So I climbed aboard bareback and headed after the guys.

I loped over to our neighbors house and found my Dad opening the gate for my brother who was out of sight and momentarily out of mind. I asked my Dad if they had found the bull. He told me that he wasn't at the neighbors any longer so my brother headed up the hill to find him.

Even at ten I knew hurt animals would usually head to water. Dad told me to head the other direction if I wanted away from my brother and his friend.

I turned Bee towards the creek and found the bull right off. He had knocked a horn off and he was ticked off to say the least. Bee had nerves of steel and headed right up to the bull. The bull turned with his good horn and caught Bee in the shoulder. Bee never faulted a bit she reached out and bit him.

The bull turned and headed towards the gate at a dead run. I trotted after him with as much pride as I had. I knew I was going to get this bull back to the corral without much hassle. I passed my Dad who had a shocked look on his face and we just kept going on to the corral.

I knew my Mom was pretty proud of me and Bee. It wasn't too long before my brother and his friend came riding in on their motorbikes. It was neat to hear my Mom and Dad both tell him that his ten-year-old sister got the bull in by herself.

To say the least it took him years to live that down. Bee and I had many more adventures and I loved my days with her.

I always say every horse has its day and every horse has its final day. That day came in the form of a night. I was twelve or thirteen that fall and I remember dreaming of a big white horse with wings flying down off the mountains and just as that big white horse almost hit me I woke up.

I remember waking up with such a start that I actually hit my head on the bunk bed. I couldn't get back to sleep and something didn't feel quite right so I slipped out of the window and headed down to the horse corral.

When I reached the gate I saw the worst sight I had ever seen, all the horses were gathered around Bee as she lay on the ground. I screamed and flew over the fence to her side. I pulled her head up onto my knee and cried as her breathing shallowed and stopped.

I sat in the horse corral until daylight, but just before the sun came up, I am pretty sure I witnessed a miracle or my mind was playing tricks on me. Either way it was something I will never forget.

As I sat with Bee the other horses gathered around me and as daylight approached. I heard a horse in the distance whinny and all my horses joined in. That in itself wasn't weird except we had no neighbors with horses to whinny and what I heard was close.

It may be just wishful thinking but to this day I swear the whinny came from that white horse I dreamed of and he was an angel sent to retrieve Bee.

I have heard when you see winged horses that heaven is waiting for you. When I die I am sure my winged horse will be Bee.

A New Horse

The ugliest horse I had ever seen was a two-year-old starved and horribly neglected little sorrel mare. I was ten-years-old when she came to our ranch. She was so skinny that her backbone stuck up a good inch or so, and her head looked four times the size of her body. The bone structure on this little mare was light, to say the least. When she walked, she practically dragged her head on the ground. Pride was just one of the things that she lacked.

I asked my grandfather why he brought her home. He explained that all of the mare's ugliness was just top-dressing. With a little food and love, she would become a great-looking little horse. With my mare, Bee, being twenty-five and arthritic, he thought I would soon need a new horse.

The truth had finally surfaced, Grandpa expected that runty little stitch of a horse to be the replacement for my fourteen-hundred pound, foundation bred, topnotch roping horse mare Bee. I wanted nothing to do with that ugly little wannabe replacement.

I ignored the little mare for two years. I refused to catch her for anyone to ride. I didn't want anyone to even see her on our place. I would give Bee a can of grain and stay to make sure she ate all of it. But I never paid any attention to whether the little sorrel mare got all of her food, or if the other ranch horses chased her away before she could finish eating.

I worked odd jobs to buy minerals and vitamins for Bee, but I never gave any to the little sorrel mare. Heck, I didn't even name her at that time, she was just known as that the little sorrel mare. Later, she turned out to be quite a little riding horse, but she was too small for the adults, so mostly, my brother rode her.

Looking back now, I would have taken a strap to myself for treating any living thing with so little compassion. I was a cruel and hateful pre-teen to say the least. I never hit or starved the mare. I just refused to give her her what I could have easily given; nutrients and love.

One night, while I sat out in the pasture holding Bee's head in my arms, her eyes closed for the last time, it all changed. I cried long into the night, refusing to leave Bee's side, until my father buried her the following morning. The veterinarian told my father that Bee's death was due to old age. Her heart had just given up. The vet's words were hard for me to believe. One thing that Bee never did was to give up.

Bee could keep up with any horse, gaited or not. She loved me like her own child. And I loved her more than any child loves her mother. She was my babysitter while my parents worked. She protected me when my brother and his friends picked on me. At the time of her death I was ten-years-old and devastated over losing the best friend I had ever known.

As I watched Dad take Bee's body away the next morning I collapsed in the horse corral, crying for the rides I would never have with her again. I had to accept the fact that I could no longer tell all my problems to Bee anymore or look into her soft, brown eyes and know everything would be all right. I swore I would never own a horse again or ride one for as long as I lived!

Suddenly a soft, caring, little wet nose nudged me. Because I was so upset, I didn't think about how much I disliked that little sorrel mare. When she tried to comfort me, I turned and buried my face into her neck and sobbed. She just stood there, and in her own a way, gave me a hug.

We stayed in the horse corral together for most of the day. She never walked away from me, she listened to all my problems and even contributed a few of hers. In her eyes, I saw her love for me and realized how much she needed my love. To this day, I still would swear that I saw a tear in her eye for Bee.

Forgetting my vow to never ride or own another horse as long as I lived, and because of the kindness the sorrel mare had shown, I decided to start riding her.

Soon, we were inseparable and went everywhere together. I would skip school and take her up to the meadow to eat. I bought every vitamin and mineral they made for helping horses to grow and everything else I could afford to make her life better. I still couldn't think of a good enough name for her so I continued to call her *"The Little Sorrel Mare."* However, the *little* part of her nickname was vanishing rapidly. I spent the whole summer running wild with the sorrel mare. I called her "Sorrel" for short. Now when I look back, that was the best summer of my life, not many compare to it. I still missed Bee terribly, but I knew she had taught the sorrel all she could.

I started showing her in 4H and at a Junior Rodeo. Grandpa told me I needed a name for the sorrel so that she could hold her head up as we entered the arena and they said our names, but nothing seemed to fit her, nothing seemed good enough for her.

She beat everybody at barrels and poles. She was wonderful with her quick turns and fast take offs. We dreamed of being barrel racers when we grew up if we ever grew up, Sorrel seemed to have a slight smile on her face when ever we would win an event.

Calf-roping was a cinch with a quick little horse like Sorrel under me. However, I could never tie goats. The first time she saw a goat, she came to a sudden stop and just stared at it for the longest time, she wouldn't budge.

Sorrel marched in parades. She was getting big, her sleek body glistened in the sun as she would prance down the highway in front of everybody, She would arch her neck and prance as if she were carrying the Queen of England. We traveled all over our mountain for a ten mile circumference take to the mountains for days on end and then down to town for an ice cream bar for two summers with no hassles or problems.

I felt safe and secure on my new best friend. Even though she still had no name except "Sorrel."

A Deep Hole

One fall, while chasing cows up in the high pasture. Sorrel and I ran through some thick brush, trying to get around a cow, when suddenly Sorrel came to an abrupt stop. I thought maybe she was getting a little tired, so I promised her as soon as we turned the cow, we could rest. But we had to keep moving right now. The cows were getting away. I knew that if I lost track of them in the brush and timber, it would be hard to find them again, without tracking.

I kicked Sorrel and tried to get her moving. Every time I kicked, she would nip my leg. I started to get off to lead her. Again, she turned and nipped my leg. She was acting so weird -- all stretched out and refusing to move a foot. She was pulling brush out by the roots. She must have pulled about six bushes out before I could she what she saw. We were straddling a fifteen-foot-deep mine hole that was about six-feet across. Long before I was ever thought of my Grandfather told me that the land was mined and they dug holes everywhere. I had always been warned to watch out for them but they already had twelve holes staked out and I knew where they were this one was never staked the brush was so thick that it wasn't able to be seen and it was in a place we seldom go, no roads led there.

I had no clue if we were going to be able to jump over the hole. Sorrel had propped her front feet up on a log that had fallen over it. Her back feet were barely on its edge. Visions of my parents finding us lying dead at the bottom of this old mine hole flashed thought my head. Sorrel stood straight up on her hind feet and spun around until we were clear of the hole. I walked her the whole way home. She deserved a huge break and I knew she was tired, a long walk with a nice loosened cinch was just what she needed. Besides, I was shaking so much I was not sure I could have stayed on to ride her home. I knew I had found a kindred sprit in the sorrel, and I had found that one great horse that you only find once in your life.

At last, I came up with a name for the little sorrel. I called her Gadjet, after Inspector Gadjet, the cartoon hero who could invent gadgets to save himself and others. The name, "Gadjet," fit because of all the nifty ways she knew for getting us out of tight fixes. In addition to saving us from falling into the mine hole she also got me out of a lot of chores around the house. I would sneak out and climb on Gadjet and head for the hills when Mom would tell me to do dishes. I promised Gadjet I would always take care of her, as she had taken care of me. I told her that I would make sure no one ever separated us.

About a year later, we were riding home at one in the morning, from my best girlfriend's house. Without warning, Gadjet darted to the left, out from under a tree, and took off running. I tried to slow her down. I was bareback and carrying my backpack with a baby bunny I had found hurt along the trail in it. Gadjet took hold of the bit and kept running. I held on for dear life.

I heard something thumping the ground behind us. In the moonlight I could see a form chasing us. I couldn't quite make out what it was until we crossed the open meadow. Then I saw a cougar my heart kept beat with the pounding of his feet behind us, my imagination saw him way better than my eyes did, long and sleek with his pearly white teeth wanting the taste of horse, baby bunny and girl flesh.

We had another mile until we reached the flat fields by our house. I didn't know if Gadjet could keep up this pace long enough. She ran for all she could down that mountain, over rocks and trees. Only God knows what else she maneuvered around that night. The cougar finally stopped chasing us, and we made it safely home -- Gadjet, baby bunny, and me.

Down Hill

Well a man once told me that when a person goes downhill they are done for. Well I went downhill and very quickly and in those few short seconds I was sure I was done for. This is one of those stories that hurt then and hurts even now, but not quite as much.

I was thirteen and my Dad told me we had a bull with a broken leg up on the hill behind our house. He said I needed to get on Gadget and go get him, so I did as I was told for maybe the second time in my life. I saddled my horse, grabbed a lariat and filled my canteen. I was a cowgirl and was bound and determined to prove I was better than any man living or dead.

After riding about two hours or so I found him under a tree by the watering hole at the top of a steep incline or decline looking down. I got off and assessed my situation a large bull and a little barely thousand pound mare, and me with more guts than sense. No problem, I would rope him, tie him to my saddle horn and lead him down the mountain (just like in the movies). ThenI would stop for a drink of water, maybe once (because it sounded like something John Wayne would do), and be home before lunch.

I figured I would tell my story around the lunch table of how I roped him and my horse pulled with all her might. I would have to tell them how hot it was, we had to stop and get a drink, maybe I would say I emptied my canteen and had to drink out of a hoof print to stay alive. I am sure that would definitely rate an ice cream bar after lunch. I couldn't wait to get home and tell my story.

His horns made an easy target for my loop and once I had him caught I proceeded to tie him to my saddle horn. My little horse was just an amature at the tender age of three, I had never roped anything off of her before. But Bee was getting old and I hated to use her for hard jobs like this.

The bull weighed about twenty-two hundred pounds with big curved horns; in short he looked like the devil with a broken leg.

We were able to pull the bull out from under the tree and start down the road but it was hot and he was belligerent and sore. Our going was much slower than I had planned, if he didn't hurry up I would be lucky if I got home by dinner.

I fought that danged bull for about an hour and a half and we only made about two hundred yards of progress. Temperatures were well above ninety degrees and my canteen was almost empty, with still a long ways to go. My horse was sweating and I was matching every drop. I got off and pulled her for a few feet.

It was no use we were going to have to try something else, I got back on and got behind him and tried to scare him. He walked a few feet and then turned and charged, we turned to run, and he was right on our tails. He wasn't letting up and we weren't slowing down. We turned and headed straight down the mountain at a run with him in close pursuit, bellowing and throwing snot.

Now we were moving, I realized I might actually make it down by lunch and boy howdy now I had a really good story. My little mare never missed a step running down that mountain. The bull was getting tired, but for some reason that was just making him madder. I turned a corner and realized, with horror, that I had closed the main gate (according to my neighbor, never in my life did I close the first gate). How the heck was I going to get it open without getting killed.

The same time that thought flashed through my head so did my whole life and my horse seemed to be flying. I looked down she was flying through the air, I am not quite sure what I thought was happening, but I didn't think that the bull had just came up between her hind legs and tossed her and me. When I realized what was happening, I tried frantically to undo the rope so my horse could get free from the bull, but it was wrapped so many times and pulled so tight that I couldn't get it free.

We hit the ground with the bull right on top of us. I realized he was going to kill my horse if I didn't get her free so I reached down and unlatched my back cinch followed by my front one, the next few seconds flew by. Gadjet was back on her feet heading down the mountain, the bull right on her tail and me, with my foot caught in the stirrup, bouncing behind him.

A broken legged bull was no match for the fear in those three-year-old legs; she left him behind without any trouble. I was working on freeing my leg when I realized the bull had just plowed through a fence. Oh, how I hate barbed wire. I tried frantically to free myself but my leg was stuck and all the bouncing around was making it almost impossible to concentrate.

I remembered my pocket knife and started to saw on the rope connecting my saddle to the devil. Rocks, trees, and bushes seemed to jump out from everywhere all of them with one thing in mind, me. I swear I saw a smile on his face every time I hit something, I am sure he swerved to make sure I hit some of them.

With a snap I was free and that devil just kept on going. I laid back with my aching body resting on the ground. Finally the world had stopped spinning and I think that is when I started breathing again.

I heard a rig headed up the mountain it was Mom. "I saw Gadjet running for the barn. Are you okay?" I got in the pickup and turned to look into her worried face.

I knew I had the greatest story to tell but I busted a lot more than bones that day...my pride was split right down the center. I sat quietly for some time trying to decide what to tell her. But in the end I just turned and said in my most nonchalant voice, "I really would rather not talk about it, if you don't mind."

What a day!

The Slide

Four years ago during fall round up, I was riding Gadjet the rough country while chasing a group of cows down a shale slide. Gadjet stopped and tried to go backwards. She was having no luck. We were sliding down the side of a slick mountain, and stopping was the last thing we could do.

A string of barbed wire was strung across the bottom of the mountain, beneath the rocks. Gadjet slid into the wire. It caught on her hind feet. She tried with all her might to stay in one place. I got off of her but slid halfway down the mountain on the shale rock. I was able to inch my way back up the mountain to her and break her loose from the barbed wire. I had no fence pliers with me so I had to twist the barbed wire back and fourth in my hands until it snapped.

Together, we slid the rest of the way down the mountain. All I could do was to try and stay ahead of her. I checked her out at the bottom, figuring she would be cut to pieces, but she had no blood or cuts whatsoever.

Most horses would have freaked out in that situation and be badly cut. I hate to think what would have happened to me if Gadjet had panicked. But, when I am sitting atop one of the best little cow horses I have ever met, I know that I am safe and sound from whatever might come our way.

Growing up, I worried about letting Gadjet down. My life evolved around her.

She taught me compassion, among other things. Love and beauty doesn't have to be seen by others and it really is only skin deep. and most of all made my Grandfathers words sink in, with a good horse under you there isn't nothing you can't accomplish. When I became a teenager, I never drank or did drugs. I knew she would know. I am very grateful to the gentle and trusting nature of that little sorrel mare.

In the days since her retirement from hard riding, Gadjet has taught many children to ride with confidence. When she competes at the fair with a child, everybody knows her name and that most likely, the child who is riding her will win anything they enter. I have been offered a lot of money for Gadjet, but I would never sell her. She will live out her days on our cattle ranch. She has earned the reward of being cared for in her old age.

I want the rest of the world to know about the little sorrel mare who has touched the lives of hundreds in our community and saved mine three times. She may not be registered, but to those who know her, she is the most well bred little horse in the world. She never did get very large, but she has the biggest heart of any horse you will ever have the pleasure of sitting astride.

We tried to have Gadjet bred, but with no luck. I guess you just can't duplicate a miracle. So Gadjet has gotten old and when she leaves us, her line will end. I fear the day will soon be upon us when I have to hold her for the last time. As I did with Bee so many years ago, I will have to say good-bye to one of the best friends I ever had.

I often wonder what would have happened had Grandpa not seen the good in that scrawny little sorrel mare. I tell my husband that when they bury me, to put an apple in the coffin with me, so that I can give it to Gadjet when I see her again. For I know that there has to be a heaven for good horses.

Another Angel

As with every good horse that touches so many lives when they leave this world they are greatly missed. Gadjet grew up in rodeo arenas and it was fit that when she passed on it was with five hundred people watching and crying.

On August 23, 2008, that day came. It was the Saturday Night PRCA Rodeo at our local fair. The stands were just starting to fill up with onlookers. I sat on the sidelines and watched as the Rodeo Princess warmed Gadjet up for her run in the grand entry. One more child she was teaching to ride.

The princess rode Gadjet over to where I stood watching and with a hint of surprise explained, "Gadjet only wanted to run," that night.

I told her the old girl knew her business and her business was speed and rodeos, so just sit back and enjoy. She turned and started Gadjet back down the fence towards the bucking chutes when I saw Gadjet waver ever so slightly. I stood up knowing something wasn't right. Gadjet took about ten more steps and wavered again.

I jumped the fence and yelled for the Princess to get off her. I saw Gadjet look over to where I was running across the arena and she started to me panic showed in her face.

She fell side ways and a couple cowboys held her down so she didn't hurt me as she was still trying to get to me. As I reached her I dropped down beside her and held her head in my lap. I yelled for some of the guys to strip the tack off her and for someone to get a vet.

I could tell she was leaving me and I cried like a baby begging her not to die in the middle of the arena while hundreds of people watched in horror. A barricade of horses were brought in to shield the sight from the onlookers. Cowboys and cowgirls lined up on their trusty mounts and watched in horror as mine fought for her life.

Her gums were white and I yelled again for a vet. When the vet showed she checked her vitals and informed me she had most likely had a heart attack and would be dead in a very short while.

I asked her to make her last few minutes comfortable for her. I talked to Gadjet as her eyes glassed over and her breathing stopped. I collapsed onto her neck in a frenzy of tears.

I heard other people crying and looked up to find hats off heads and heads bent low. The announcer was silent as he stood in the arena with his microphone in hand and watched. Bull riders watched from the top of the chutes, a horse whinnied and more joined in from somewhere in the barns.

I was drug off of her and watched as a bunch of cowboys carried her into the back of a trailer. One young cowboy turned to me and somewhere amongst the mix of all this I found a family of friends.

The young cowboy said to me. "When a good equine athlete dies, they deserve to be carried into the trailer not hauled by a tractor."

The princess looked at me with tears in her eyes and said sorry for killing Gadjet. I hugged her and let her know it wasn't her fault. I should have known that a strong horse like Gadjet would go out with style, it wasn't in her to grow old and die in the pasture.

Given the chance to go out to pasture or to jump in the trailer and go to another rodeo you wouldn't even have to put a halter on her. She would have jumped in the trailer in a heartbeat.

I took her home and buried her below the house in the meadow she used to live in. I cut a hunk of main from her and had a shoe pulled off of her for a memento.

I set her bridle in the grave with her. No horse I figure will ever be good enough to ever wear her bridle.

A Marble monument was ordered and placed on the spot where she will rest for eternity. It reads:

Gadjet

1986 to August 23rd, 2008
Gone But Never Forgotten

On the darkest of nights when the valley is still and quiet. I swear I can hear her hoof beats for I know they are forever imprinted in my heart. Heaven has received yet another angel.

Lucky Lace Bug

What a name, but that was her name, Lucky Lace Bug and it fit her to a "T." At three o'clock on the morning of February 24th of 2004, I was awaken by a phone call. A frantic lady on the other end asked if I was Dawn Nelson and if I loved horses as much as she had heard. I assured her at three o'clock in the morning that was the only thing I did love.

Well she continued in somewhat of a panicked voice. "I have a yearling bay roan filly who was attacked by a cougar her mother was killed and she was badly injured."

I sat straight up in bed knowing an injured horse would need a vet so I immediately told her a good one's name and number.

"No," she said, "that isn't what she needs. She needs a new home within the next hour."

"Why," I asked, "would it be so time impairative? How bad is she?" While this lady asked me if I loved horses, the worst pictures ran through my head of this poor filly almost dead or bleeding to death. I lived almost three hours away. What on earth was she thinking?

"Well," she continued, "I have been on vacation for two months and she was left in the barn to heal."

That didn't sound that bad to me, in fact I would most likely put her in a nice straw lined stall and baby her too. I still didn't understand what the time of one hour had to do with anything. Obviously she should be mostly healed with two months of doctoring and tending to.

Finally my patience wearing thin I yelled, "Lady why is it so dang imperative that I be there within the hour?"

"Well," she stammered, "while I was gone for two months, nobody fed or watered her at all. She is barley alive...I think. Some people were here and saw her and they just went to call the police and turn me in for animal cruelty."

That didn't sound like a bad idea, but I knew she was as worried about the filly's welfare right now as I was. She informed me she had someone who was supposed to have fed and cared for her but they got thrown in jail and never told anybody about the filly being locked in the wood stall.

I knew what I was going to see when I got there was going to be bad. There was no way I could have made it there in an hour no matter how fast I drove, but as luck would have it, my parents lived about a half an hour from her. I woke my parents up and informed them what was going on.

My father who has never been a true horse lover jumped out of bed and into the truck to go get her and take her to the vet. I had already called and relayed the story to the vet and had her waiting on the filly's arrival.

I jumped in the my pickup and hooked up the trailer and headed for a long morning's drive to go see how bad this little bay roan filly really was. When I arrived at the vet's office I was informed that she was badly dehydrated and malnourished most likely beyond repair.

I was pulled aside and quietly informed that it would be kinder to put her down than to try to make her live if she even could. The vet said she had cocked ankles that most likely would not straighten out. She was walking on the bones in her ankles not on her hooves.

My Dad said he had to lift her into the truck as she could not walk at all. He covered her with blankets to keep in what body heat she did have. He said he didn't think she had much hope of surviving and being normal.

I stepped from the vet's office not sure what I was going to do. If she was that bad off maybe the kindest thing to do was to put her down. As we neared the vet's barn I heard a faint whinny coming from inside, my heart leaped I had never heard her whinny before but I knew in my heart it had to be her.

As we made our way to her stall I heard it again, I expected to find her standing and looking at me for help but what I saw was horrible. Laying on a thick blanket of straw was the tiniest yearling I had ever seen weighing barley three-hundred pounds when other siblings her age weighed close to eight or nine-hundred pounds.

Her eyes followed me but her body refused her subtle attempts to get up. Her eyes were sunk into her face like a skeleton. Her skin hung to her bones and sagged under her jaw. Her breathing was so faint I wasn't sure she was breathing. She had horrible mats in her hair in some spots the hair had actually pulled out in clumps and left open sores.

I felt my eyes mist up as I stood there looking at this poor, unloved and sorely neglected young horse. I knelt down and stroked her neck she looked right at me with her left eye as if begging for help.

"What can I do for you?" I whispered. She lifted her head ever so slightly and rested her nose on my leg. I ran my hand down her cold black nose and to my surprise she opened her mouth and licked my hand.

I had to admit she had more heart than sense looking at her she should have been dead, but she was still fighting, so why couldn't I help her fight her fight.

"No," I said, "I will not put her down, if she wants to die she is going to have to do it all on her own because I am going to try my dangest to save her...no matter what."

The veterinarian helped me fashion some leg braces for her back legs out of PVC pipe, gauze and vet wrap. It didn't look half bad for an early morning attempt at homemade braces.

I backed my trailer up to the barn and we loaded her in, covered her in blankets and hot water bottles. I drove her home stopping every twenty-miles or so to check on her and try to get her to drink a little water.

She never moved the whole drive home and she never even attempted any water. On the way home, I have to admit, I cried at he shear fact that anyone could treat an animal that bad. I knew it wasn't the lady's fault. She hadn't known the guy had been sent to jail.

I called my husband and asked him to bed a stall down in the barn for her and get the feeding tubes ready along with some chopped hay and grain.

At this point, he had no idea what a project I was bringing home in the back of my trailer. I was prepared to put her on an IV if we had to. The vet informed me that I may have to fashion a sling from the barn ceiling to help her stand and take the pressure off the ankles. I was prepared to do whatever was needed to help her survive.

As I pulled into the drive everyone came out to see what I had brought home. I opened the trailer and I saw everyone's faces drop, but mine lit up she was standing bracing herself against the side of the trailer, the braces we had fashioned were working.

My husband and I carried her into the barn and set her on the ground. She immediately stood up, wobbly, everyone asked why I even brought her home.

Everyone that is except my husband who just helped in every way imaginable and cursed anyone who could do this to an animal.

She drank about a half of a cup of water that night and nuzzled the hay but never even opened her mouth. I knew it was a small leap for her. I was as happy as if she had ran around and gobbled up everything in sight.

I slept next to her that night and offered her water and grain every chance I could. She didn't eat much, but I still remember the first real bite of grain she took three days later, so carefully as if she was afraid it might disappear. She licked the grain and then opened her mouth and took a small bite and then a bigger bite and then she just gobbled up about a half a can of grain. I ran to the house and told my husband all about it.

The days of February seemed to creep by. She began to eat a little more then a little more. By the end of February her skin was a little tighter and her feet were working better. She could stand for about an hour without her braces before she would collapse onto her bones again.

I named her Lace because of her delicate condition. When she came, just like a fine stitch of lace, she was delicate and pretty. Long hours brushing her coat gotout most of the caked on manure and mats of hair.

We took her to the shop and gave her a warm bath to get rid of the lice, along with the rest of the dirt and grime so we could properly take care of the sores on her skin. Lace was coming along better than anyone believed she ever would. She was the sweetest little horse I had ever met.

She could barley walk, but she could and she would always meet us at the barn entrance. She would let us pet and play with her for hours if we wanted to. During this time she earned the Bug part of her name. She was becoming the biggest pest ever known to man; no gates could hold her in. She would just slip by them and soon she was standing next to the grain bin looking for more, which we always gave her.

Our next big milestone was on March 4th. Every morning when the sun would shine, I would turn Lace Bug out in a run and let her walk around, always hoping that her energy would pick up and she would run or buck or play. I was always a little disappointed at the fact that she hadn't seemed to want to run and play like the other yearlings who were running in the next pen over.

On this morning, I turned her out and even though she looked a little fatter and healthier she still just barely walked around the pen. Her head hung low and she looking so worn out. I turned and walked back inside to clean out her stall when I heard a loud thud. Then to my surprise Lace came running back inside and right to me.

My heart skipped a beat she had gone from almost dead to running with in one month. I knew I was looking at a miracle, maybe the only one I would ever know in my life. She would began to make laps around her run every morning with just wrap on her ankles. She was getting so strong and beautiful.

I had no clue what I was ever going to do with Lace Bug. She was extremely stunted and would most likely never be able to hold anyone on her back. Come summer we turned her out in pasture with some other yearling becoming two-year-olds her age. She was dwarfed by a good two-feet by almost every one of them.

She fattened up and filled out but never really grew much taller through the spring or summer. I figured I had a very small filly that might never even be tall enough to even make into a broodmare. She was not papered either so, basically, I just had a pasture ornament.

June came and so did a letter in the mail from the vet. It seemed the woman who had originally owned her wanted to know if she had lived and how she was doing. I gave her a call and informed her of her health and how she was and that she was filling out nicely.

She again thanked me for taking her and just before she hung up she said, "Oh, and by the way, could I get your address? I would like to send her application for registration to you."

I couldn't believe it! Lace Bug had the ability to be a registered quarterhorse. Maybe she did have a life as a broodmare ahead of her.

I received the papers not more than a week later, I crossed out the names the lady had given her and wrote in one of my own. "Lucky Lace Bug" and low and behold six-months later I received her full papers.

She had good bloodlines, some of the best I had seen on paper. My little bay roan filly with her only markings being her cougar scars was turning out to be heaven sent.

It is amazing what time makes you forget. I forgot the endless hours of waiting and praying that she would get better and heal properly. Wishing she was papered only to find out she was, naming her and loving her.

I got so busy with breeding other mares and trying to make a living out of horses that I forgot one very important thing. The fact that God could change our lives with one small lump.

I had been holding a small secret to myself until it grew large enough to worry about. After seeing a doctor he informed me that I most likely had just months to live and that this time next year I probably would not be here.

In the fall of 2005, I regretfully placed Lace Bug up for sale with a "good home only" clause along with many other horses I had and loved. I never told anyone, even my husband, about the doctor appointments. I told him it was just regular check ups.

So I picked up a contract supplying horses to the Border Patrol. I knew it wouldn't make me immortal but it did keep my mind off of the situation at hand. I entered a few writing contests and spent the days riding in at the neighbors indoor arena. He was the first person I confided in with the doctor's diagnoses, we stood and prayed right there in his indoor arena.

Shortly after that I told my husband and went in for another doctor's appointment to figure out the next move. The doctor was baffled. The lump, it seemed was just that, a lump. Not cancerous, as he originally told me. It still needed to be removed but I knew I had just seen my second miracle. A tinge of sadness came with my miracle however, I had sold off three of my favorite horses.

The third came in the fall of 2006 just after I had a bilateral mastectomy, a call came from the lady who bought Lace Bug.

She said she no longer could keep her and was going to place her up for sale, but had decided some reason to call me first.

I had no money to buy her back at that time so I told her with tears in my eyes to place her up for sale. She called me back two days later with a new idea.

"Lacey wants to come back to you," She said. "Do you have any broke or started geldings you would like to trade for her?"

Yes, I did have one that was a little too laid back for the Border Patrol. So I told her about him and she said drop him off, we can do a trade.

I drove the three hours to drop him off and see my little Lace Bug. As we walked to the barn I heard that dear little whinny again and I knew that she heard me.

I believe everything in life happens for a reason, Lace Bug will be a broodmare on this ranch for many years to come, she will have a lifetime home here. This is obviously where she was meant to be, for she has found her way here twice and now she is home.

Pain Cow

We called her, "Pain Cow." She was a big yellow cow with a white face and weighed close to fifteen hundred pounds, and it all started with a dead calf.

Pain Cow had just given birth to a still born at 2:00 A.M. My Dad rushed into my room to tell me I had to get Bee and get Pain Cow into the barn so we could put a new baby on her.

I crawled out of bed and went to catch Bee but, thanks to my bad luck, she did not want to be caught. I didn't want to run around outside on twenty acres in December at 2:00 A.M. and try to find her. So I caught Chief, a three-year-old appaloosa I had just acquired. I climbed aboard him bareback. He wasn't very well broke yet, but he would have to do and I hated saddles.

The darkness seemed to engulf us as we rode along. All was going well until my Dad turned the corner with a light and came up behind us causing Chief's shadow to fall in front of him. The monsters suddenly came out of the night, full force, and their snarling mouths were coming straight for him, or so he thought.

He jumped straight up to the stars. I still swear I saw a UFO and touched the moon before we landed. He swerved left but another monster must have jumped out, he suddenly flipped right, then he lost his footing and we fell hard. When I realized it was my head spinning and not the world, I turned to the strange sound coming from my Dad's truck; laughter. He was laughing at me, the nerve.

After cussing a little and limping around a bit I jumped back on. We chased that cow up one side of the field and down the other. Finally Dad said go get Bee and rope her we'll drag her home (great now I was supposed to be able to rope a charging cow in the dark). After getting Bee saddled, I was back at it. By now it was almost daylight and I was tired and cranky.

I threw a loop and missed, dang it! Okay so, "dang it" wasn't what I said. Finally after a couple tries, I caught her and dallied her to my horn just like the cowboys did in all those movies. Then I heard the worst sound a cowboy or, in this case- girl, would ever hear...SNAP! My cinch broke. I was flying across the snow covered ground still astride my saddle but Bee was missing.

By this time I was wide awake and I was determined to get this cow. Dad tried to drive over the rope to stop her but it didn't work. I just managed to slide right underneath the pickup. Dad drove up beside me and asked what I thought. Gee, I'm tied to a saddle and flying behind a cow, what am I supposed to think? Help!!!

I was watching him so closely that I didn't realize she was headed for a fence;

one post ....

two posts ....

three posts ....

Owww!!!!

Something caught on the barbed wire. The saddle flipped over and I lost my seat and went sailing off the back. Dad finally got the rope tied to the bumper of the truck and I was able to catch Bee. Dad tried to drag Pain Cow behind the pickup while Bee and I tried to get her moving.

Well most people and animals you will ever run across will always have one thing in common, stubbornness. And between that cow and my father I still don't know which one won that day but I do know I lost.

It all seemed to happen rather quickly; the cow stopped waking and fell down then I told Dad to stop the truck so I could loosen the rope. He did and the next thing I knew I was flying through the air. I took out a string of barbed wire with my leg and was flung up against a post. Pain Cow was mad, she had her head rammed up against my legs pushing me even harder into the post. Everything seemed to be happening in slow motion; at least from my point of view.

Finally, after a few seconds or minutes, I couldn't tell, Pain Cow backed off and I was able to crawl out into the snow. My leg hurt so badly I couldn't bend it. My jeans were ripped to shreds and so were my legs. I crawled into the pickup and Dad told me to drive slowly he would follow her and lead Bee.

Ha! I drove so fast that she practically swung around corners, all the while Dad yelling at me to slow down before I killed her. Not that I would have cared.

Afterall, she tried to kill me, I was just returning the favor.

Later we got a calf grafted on to her and Dad told me I could have that danged yellow and white face. That's how she so gracefully got her name that day; "Pain Cow."

Pain Cow's Demise

After she tore up my knee and almost killed me, Pain Cow was given to me by my father. She raised three calves from the day she was given to me to the day she met her demise.

We had turned Pain Cow out to pasture that spring with her steer calf. Dad, Mom, or me would drive the pasture every week or so to see how everyone was.

It was the beginning of October when we got a call from the Sheriff's Department. As usual, for us, we were at home watching a John Wayne movie.

Seems one of our cows was dead in the middle of the road. We were told and we needed to get her moved quickly.

We rushed off to find our dead cow. Mom went in her car, Dad and I in the pickup.

We drove every road county and state around our pasture trying to find the cow with no luck. My Mom finally went down and called the Sheriff's Department to find out exactly where the cow was.

She came back with the story that it was in our pasture. Why we had to move her quickly, I had no clue.

We drove the pasture roads; lo and behold, we found the cow. It was Pain Cow. However, she was laying funny so my Dad did a little investigating and found evidence of a small caliber bullet hole in her head. I was irked, to say the least.

I jumped in my Dad's truck with my Mom riding shotgun and we went scouting the local camps for a matching weapon.

Three camps later, we pulled up to an all male camp. My Mom looked at me and expressed her dislike in walking into a camp full of drunken men.

Not me. I stepped out of the truck and marched right into the camp. Some men stood up and came towards me.

"Which one of you bastards killed my cow?" I asked. Mom said it wasn't a real good approach. One ugly man smiled and asked what I was planning on doing to the killer.

"Kill him." I replied. I heard my Mom gasp next to me.

"How?" He asked.

"Are you the killer?"

"Maybe." He said while reaching for his gun.

I knew I had found the bastard I was searching for. I felt like Billy The Kid or Jesse James in some out-west showdown. All I had was a pistol holstered on my hip. So like in the movies I pulled back the flap on my coat and unsnapped my holster.

The man stopped, his face dropped and he asked, "You think I did it? Get the #$#@ out of our camp!"

"No! You get the #$^@ off my range." I demanded.

Then he asked me if I was for real, if I would really shoot someone for shooting a cow. The funniest thing is, before I had the chance to answer my Mom burst in.

"Mister, she has been known to do a lot of thing her father and I don't approve of." My Mom stopped and looked from him to me and continued, "But this isn't one of them."

Well obviously, you have figured out I never shot him and he never shot me, and Pain Cow's death was never solved. One thing I learned; parents may be a real pain in the hind end sometimes, but when you are in a showdown they are always there to back you up.

Forty Dollar Pig

My husband and I had been married about a year when my Dad gave me a bottle pig. She was so cute. She was the runt of the litter so they pulled her off her mother and I got her.

I carried her home in a small cat carrier. On the way home, I was a little worried as to what my husband would say but, when I arrived, he was understandable to the baby pig's circumstances. We made a small pen outside the house for this little gal and tried putting a dog harness on her and staking her out so she could play in the yard.

She slipped out of the harness many times and we played a lot of "chase the wild pig." I had a dog we called Diamond. She was not much of a people dog but she loved this damn pig. She would go out in the fields, kill gophers, and bring them to the pig to eat.

We named the rapidly growing pig Brandi. She ate with the dog; she slept with the dog, and worst of all she traveled with the dog. She would walk across the fields after Diamond, and when Brandi got tired, she would lay down. My husband and I would get the call from a worried neighbor about Brandi laying in the creek just down the road a mile or two.

So off we would go with the pickup, find her, throw her in the back, and drive home. During this time I bought two baby bottle lambs just because I had always wanted a sheep and we found a calf that had lost his mother. So now, I had three animals that needed a bottle every morning.

Diamond accepted these animals into her family and made sure they all stayed together. Our phone calls started being of the content of our neighbors seeing Diamond walking down the road followed by a baby calf, two baby lambs, and bringing up the rear, was Brandi.

I can't even begin to tell you how many people would see these animals and stop to take a double look at the menagerie of critters.

By fall time the pig had grown to three hundred pounds and was one of the family she would come up to you for scratches, and would eat cookies out of your hands. She killed a few rattlesnakes and would bring them into the porch for my husband and I to see.

The baby calf had grown and was now in the replacement herd and the lambs were sold to my father. We were back to just the pig and the dog.

One hot afternoon my husband came home from changing pipes and said Brandi was down the road at the pump house and was overheated. She we jumped in a pickup and headed down to bring her home. We couldn't get her loaded into the back and so we had to pull her into the front of the cab. She laid on the front seat all the way home.

I loved the pig for one reason; whenever someone showed up who didn't know us, they would not get out of their cars because of Brandi.

When my husband's friends would get drunk at our place they would try to ride her and she would buck them off. One night a bunch of them showed up to play poker. It was cold outside so they left a case of beer on the porch. Brandi bit into and drank every single one of those beers.

I guess what this story is really leading up to is a story that happened just after she turned three. My husband and I were rounding up cattle in one of our pastures and I had to go to work that evening so I headed home to get cleaned up.

I opened the truck door and was surprised to see our house door open. I walked inside and saw my house was turned upside down. My desk was tipped over. The dinner table was upside down. All of my dishes were in a broken pile on the floor. My refrigerator door was swung open and food was pulled out.

At first, I thought maybe Brandi had broken in until I saw our money jar broken and money everywhere. I quickly dialed 911 and grabbed my pistol from the overhead shelf inside the door. After making sure it was loaded, I reported to the operator what I was finding in my home.

I explained to the woman that my house looked like a tornado hit it. I told her I had a gun and I was going to walk through the house to make sure no one was in there. She said she could send police cars and if I wanted, I could wait.

I put her on speakerphone and headed through the house. The TV looked like someone had grabbed it and tossed it. Our stereo was pulled out and tipped over. The couches, too, were all tipped over.

I walked back towards the master bedroom and heard something move. It sounded like our change jar being dumped. I cocked the pistol and kicked open the door.

"Freeze!" I yelled and stopped in horror as the scene before me sunk in.

There was Brandi in the middle of our bed rooting around and making a bed for herself. She had bottles of Aleve and Tylenol bitten into and eaten.

Our house was ruined. Carpet had to come up and so did the tile in the kitchen. Our couches were ruined and Brandi laid in the back yard for weeks not feeling very good.

Two months later and over five thousand dollars worth of repairs to the house we took her to the local auction yards.

We didn't stay to watch what she brought. Less than a week later brought a shock of surprise, when the check came in the mail for her. "Forty dollars and no cents."

That is the story of my forty-dollar pig.

The Rest

Who's Afraid of A Scarecrow?

Two things that make this story a wreck from the start: we were thirteen and it was Halloween.

My friend's parents told us we were too old for trick or treating. Therefore, with some urging from my friends we decided to pull a prank. We figured it would be a great laugh at school the next day.

There were six of us that were going to go out on Halloween. We packed a bag of tricks, dressed up, and headed out.

On the way out of the driveway, I had an idea. I ran to the neighbor's corn patch and grabbed the poor old scarecrow.

First, we had to get some candy but then we went to work with the tricking. The "trick" involved a ball of twine, the scarecrow, some matches, and the town's bridge.

Everyone else waited on the shoulder of the road while me and my best friend took the stuff to the middle of the bridge. We tied the twine around the scarecrow's neck and then secured the twine to the bridge. Then we lit the scarecrow on fire and flung him over the bridge towards the water below, and took off running as fast as we could back to the waiting car.

We could hear people scream from town as our scarecrow swung over the river below and let off and eerie glow from the fire. Then we could see people running from town towards the bridge.

"Holy cow! They think someone has killed himself." My friend exclaimed as we sat watching and listening from the shoulder of the road.

"No. They think somebody murdered someone." I said as the crowd that gathered talking of police and ambulances.

"What are we going to do?" My best friend asked with evidence of fear in her voice.

We all looked at one another and realized we screwed up. We could see ambulances, lights, and fire trucks and could hear sirens coming down the road.

"Who wants to go tell them that is just a scarecrow?" One of my friends asked. Everyone answered with silence.

"I will do it." I said. I climbed from the car and shed my Halloween costume.

I remember the walk out to the center of the bridge to be a very solemn one. I kept my eyes fixed on the far side of the bridge.

As I neared the crowd, I saw many people I knew from school and from the community. I listened in horror as I heard people talking of a rescue attempt and body recovery. About that time the rope burnt through and the scarecrow fell to the small island below.

I looked over the rail at the mangled burning carcass of our scarecrow and frowned.

"Its fake." I yelled as an idea ran through my mind.

"What?" A man yelled as he looked over the bridge also.

"Yeah, look at it. It's just a scarecrow."

The crowd gasped.

"How do you know?" A woman asked.

"Well there is straw on the bridge and the rope is tied in a knot that doesn't look like it will ever come undone." I pointed to the straw that was scattered across the bridge and even on the railing.

"You know, I think she is right." A woman said. "After all it is Halloween."

"Just in case." One woman said. "Yell down and make sure it does not answer back." Everyone looked at the woman in disbelief.

The crowd dispersed and I walked back to their cars. I told all my friends that I was only going to have to do three years in jail because I told the cops their names. I let them freak out a little while until I finally told them the truth.

I guess the moral of this story is if you want to be rescued in our town you have to answer back.

Crazy Hazy

I figure "Crazy Hazy" is as close to "Henny Penny" as I could get. I am sure most of you know the story of the red chicken that gets hit on the head and thinks the sky is falling.

The chicken runs around telling everyone, "The sky is falling! The sky is falling!" If you are familiar with the story then you will understand why I think this story is a modern day retelling of Henny Penny.

In any case, I call him Crazy Hazy. Crazy, because that was obvious. Hazy, because I think with all the herbal smoking he does his head is a little hazy.

My daughter, father, and I were headed up to take a look at my cattle out on the range in August of 2008. We stopped at a local store to get some snacks and were shocked to find the door locked at ten o'clock on a Wednesday morning with the sign reading, "Open."

I knocked on the door and was immediately told that the owner would be right there. He opened the door and informed me that I had to hurry and that I could only buy ten items.

I shook my head and asked why only ten. He informed me that the economy was coming to an end and that after today the prices were going up, up, up.

"Great," I said, "maybe my beef will be worth something."

He told me, "You will have to be shooting people tomorrow to keep them from killing your cattle."

I said, "Yes, things in the economy are bad, but I don't think it is going to happen over night like you say."

"Well then you are going to lose a lot of cattle before you wake up."

I informed him as I grabbed a bag of chips and some sodas that if I lost cattle tomorrow he would be my number one suspect.

He said the police would not be working tomorrow. The government offices will be shut down and all of the postal workers will be opening up letters looking for money.

I handed him my credit card and he looked at me like I handed him a bomb.

"Hell No." He said. "I'm not getting stuck with this bill. The credit card companies are going under."

"Well I have money in my account. If you run it today, they should still be working."

He reluctantly took my credit card and then grabbed my bag of chips and held them up. "Tomorrow these will be selling for twenty dollars a bag."

I smiled and informed him, "If we didn't eat them all we would bring them back tomorrow." About that time, my father walked in carrying my daughter who needed to use the rest room.

"Oh no." He replied. "Toilet paper is on short supply right now in America. What I have is all for my usage."

My father and I laughed about this man who thought the world was ending all day. As we drove back by his store on the way home, we saw all of the signs, which stated product prices were pulled in.

His lights were off and he had gone into hiding for the end of the world. The next morning we awoke and found the sun shining and the birds chirping. As I drove home, I couldn't help but stop by and get a soda from his store.

I found the sign reading open and again the door locked. He came to the door at the first knock and opened it. I am not even sure he recognized me, because he started the same thing over about the next day.

I smiled and paid for my soda with my credit card. Again, I got to hear him spit and spatter about the failing credit card companies.

In the end of Henny Penny's story, the big bad Foxy-Woxy ate all of her friends. In Crazy Hazy's story, everyone gets to buy twenty-dollar bags of chips and eat my cows.

In conclusion, fairy tails just aren't what they used to be.

In The Crosshairs

The fall of the year I was twenty-one, my husband, who was my boyfriend at the time and I were up in the mountains helping my Dad get cows rounded up off of the range.

I was in a leg cast after I ran into a steel post on my gelding and tore the fluid sack in my knee. So, needless to say, I was doing very little real riding and a lot of pickup driving.

Dad, Mom and everyone else were hauling cows home and calves to the corral to sell. I was out on the mission of finding the bulls with my Dad's old gray pickup.

I drove to the far side of the pasture and finally found all the bulls in one group; my luck was getting better. They were on the road and wanted to move easily so I followed them nice and slow for about two miles until we turned a corner and that is when this story gets weird.

In the middle of the road sitting on a lawn chair and reading a book was a man with a gun across his lap and a bottle of whiskey laying close by. His truck was not more than ten feet away across the dirt road.

The bulls and I both took a double take. I yelled at him to please move so I could get the bulls by. He ignored me, didn't even look up. I yelled again not quite so nicely, to get out of the road. Still no response. So I honked the horn and he finally looked up. Again, I yelled, "Move out of the road!"

The sorry SOB raised his gun and pointed it at the lead bull and yelled "Get" to him. The bulls took one look at him and headed off the road and into the trees. I jumped out of the truck on crutches and tried to get them turned back, it was no use.

I tripped over a log and twisted my knee again. By this time I was so pissed I didn't care if the man had two guns, it wasn't going to stop me from giving him a large piece of my mind. As I neared the pickup the man had gone back to reading and road hunting in his lawn chair.

"You had better get out of my way or I am going to run right over the top of you!" I yelled as I jumped in the pickup and slammed the door. The glass shattered in the side window. The man picked up his lawn chair and bottle and moved to the side of the road opposite of his pickup.

I popped the truck into second gear and spun the tires heading straight between him and his truck. I shifted into third gear and then fourth. Before I got close to him, he jumped to the bank of the road as I drove by.

I reached speeds in excess of seventy miles an hour as I sped back to the corrals to grab my gelding. I jumped on him and headed back to get the bulls. As I neared the spot where the man was sitting earlier I figured he must have moved on in his great outdoor adventure and left our pasture for good. I hoped anyway.

But I was even more mad when I found he was right where I had left him. Only he had moved his chair back out to the middle of the road.

I rode right up to him and told him that I was going to go find those bulls and if he interfered again I was going to run them right over the top of him.

"Yes madam," he said as he got up and moved his chair in front of his truck.

I found the bulls just over the hills and pushed them back to the road. The man still sat on his chair in the roadway, again having moved it out in the middle of the road.

So, being a women of my words and all, I did just what I said I was going to do. I sped the bulls up to a nice run and headed them right for him. He must have thought hell was heading his way. He grabbed his bottle and dove out of his chair towards his pickup.

I ran the bulls right down the road and didn't stop until I heard him yell he was going to kill me. I turned and saw he was pointing his rifle right at me.

With no thought at all, I spun my gelding around and headed right for him, not slowing up as he collided with my horse's chest and he was flung backwards.

"You ever point a gun at me again you had better be prepared to die," I yelled as I spun my gelding over his gun and headed to the corrals.

Later that day as we were loading up horses to head home the man had the nerve to stop by camp and yell at my mother about me. My mother just told him I was very hard headed and that I didn't like guns pointed at me.

The man was obviously drunk as he stood there yelling at my mother, but he shut up real fast when my Dad, my fiancé and I came around the corner of the trailer.

He started up his truck and headed for home or the bar. One thing I know for sure about that day I might have been the one in the crosshairs but he is the one that got hit.

Incognito

When I was eighteen I spent the year working for a guest ranch close to home. I really was enjoying my days spent there. I became good friends with the cook who was also the owner's daughter.

One day the owner, who was a veterinarian, came to me and asked me if I knew the family who lived up in the mountains behind us.

"Yes, I know them." I said. "I turned their rabbits, chickens and dog loose when they forgot to feed them for a month." I knew those people only to well. They had asked my friend to feed and care for their animals while they were gone. Only they forgot to leave any food, so their animals actually started eating the other animals.

Well, the veterinarian asked if me and her daughter wanted to go check on their animals and see if they are really starving or not?

"Sure." We said. So we dressed in dark clothes and painted our faces black and headed by way of the back roads into their place. They were supposed to be gone so we were just going to say we were hunters if any one saw us.

We left the truck about two miles from their place and walked in on foot. Talking and laughing the whole time about what we looked like.

We heard dogs barking in the distance and knew that must have been their house. We circled around behind so we could come down the road beside their house and get a glimpse of the animals.

As we snuck threw the underbrush we were shocked to hear people talking. "Ssshhh," I said, "someone is home."

We snuck in a little closer and came out on the road. We started down, but to our surprise someone started shooting. We didn't know if they were shooting at us or something else.

We dove into the bushes at the side of the road and stayed hidden until we heard a rig start up and take off down the mountain.

We figured it was safe. Then we started down the road again, then we saw it.

Someone standing in the middle of the road ahead of us. Don't ask me why now, but it seemed to make sense then what we did next. We both jumped head over heels down the side of the ditch, which was actually a ten-foot ravine.

Too late, even in our camouflage clothes and paint, the guy had seen us.

"Come out," he yelled, "or I will shoot!"

I am not sure what we were thinking but we stayed hidden.

"Come out or I will call the police!" He yelled. This made me laugh because we were miles up on the top of a mountain and no one had a phone or a cell phone. My friend poked me in the ribs to keep me quiet.

"Come out!" He yelled followed by his name. I saw my opportunity to lie my way out of this fix.

I jumped up bringing my friend with me by the hand. "Oh my gosh!" I started in. "I am so glad to see you. I thought it was someone else. We are so lost." I am not sure I even took a breath between sentences. "We were hunting and got so mixed up on our directions.

"Where's your gun" He asked.

Good question. I thought

I strung out with a string of lies. He had to know was a bald face string of B.S. "We have been setting snares for rabbits. We were just headed back to the truck when we heard all the shooting and were afraid it was poachers so we hid."

"Really." He said looking straight at me.

"Yep, would I lie to you?

"I have never liked you."

"That's good." I said as we walked past him and straight down the road towards the horse pen.

"Why is that good?"

"Because I have never liked you either." I said matter of factly. We just kept on walking. As I strode past the horse pen, I looked into the sad mournful eyes of the small malnourished horse that stood eating its own manure.

"What do we do now?" I asked my friend. After thinking for a moment I said, "Tell your mother. She'll take care of it."

We walked to the pickup and drove back to the ranch. Her mother said, as a vet, these were delicate instances. Most likely, she would send some wormer and vaccinations up to them and then have someone teach them how to properly care for the animal.

I went back home to my Dad's that night. The next morning at work the people who owned the horse showed up and screamed at me.

Seems someone opened the gate and turned that poor mournful creature out to run the hills during the night and many nights to follow.

Welding Lessons

Looking back, you know how some things you did as a young kid now seemed stupid? Then there are those things that, even now, seem funny?

Well, this is one of those latter stories. I still laugh over it today when I think of the fact that I actually thought this one up myself.

I was nineteen and I had snuck into my very first bar. I had a few drinks, sang a few karaoke songs, and played a lot of pool.

Playing pool, I won one hundred dollars from some really drunk guys and that's when it happened; a song came on that I absolutely loved. So, I started dancing and after a shot of tequila, and then a couple more, I found myself dancing on the bar. Now I admit bars are for drinking on or drinking in and not for dancing. However, at that moment in my life you couldn't have convinced me of that.

I was raised in a remote mining and logging town. The people may look tough, and they are, but they know how to have a good time.

A bunch of women joined in and danced with me. Soon everyone was having a great time. When that song ended, we started another, and then another. We danced and kicked up our heels as the owners called the cops. Before long, the local police walked in.

They removed about five women from the bar counter when I realized what was happening. With little effort, I leapt off the counter, and made my way out the back door.

As I neared the alley, a guy I knew said, "Hey officer! Dawn was dancing on the counter too." Then he was spouting off a list of the other women's names.

The guy was supposed to be a friend of mine! What the heck was he doing? Three other women who had managed to get out of there joined me in the alley.

We laughed as we heard the cops haul him off to jail for being drunk in public.

"You don't want me." He said. "You want them women! Bet you don't know two of them are underage." "I will give you their names and addresses."

"Did you hear that guy rat us out to the cops?" One of the ladies asked.

"I heard." I said.

"What should we do about it?" One of the women asked.

"Next time I see him he is going to be sorry." One of the women said.

"There is no use beating him up ladies. I got a better idea." We found his truck and I taught the ladies the fun of hillbilly justice.

Three days later, the guy came back for his truck and I heard all about it from him at college the next day.

"You are never going to believe this." He started to a group of people as we sat in the lunchroom. "I got out of jail. Right? And I go to get into my truck, but my doors won't open. I never lock my doors. But I reach in my pocket and there are my keys. So, I put my key in the lock and it won't go into the keyhole. There is goo in my keyhole. Like hard goo. So, I climb in the back and go to open the slider and that's when I see it. A big rat has climbed in my truck and died on the seat."

The crowd all said, "Oh, that's gross."

"But that isn't the worst of it. The slider had stuff down the center of it and all the way around the edges of it. It won't open." He stopped and looked around the room. "Then I realized someone has messed with my truck. So I get to looking at my door better and realize that the door cracks are all filled up with the same stuff, all the way around my door. So, I end up breaking a window to get in. The smell from that rat was so bad that I almost puked. My doors were basically welded shut."

"Why would someone do that to you?" Someone in the crowd asked.

"Guess you ticked someone off." Another person stated.

"Heck, I would have done it to you had I thought of it." A seventeen-year-old guy said as he got up and headed from the room. The seventeen-year-old had gotten into an argument with him a few days earlier and ended up having his head slammed into a vending machine resulting in a broken nose.

"I would have done it too." Another guy said. "You are mean to everyone here."

I listened and smiled inwardly. I didn't realize how mean this guy had been to everyone there and how much everyone had wished they had given him the welding lesson.

A Lost Soul

A friend and I drove to Spokane for the day with our monthly paychecks. They weren't much, even combined, but they were ours.

We had to do some grocery shopping and then we were going to go to a tack store and look at horse tack. I was seventeen and I had never seen an actual tack store; at least not one that was dedicated to just horse equipment. I was thrilled.

We left early in the morning, figuring to catch breakfast in Colville and be in Spokane by ten. With no excitement or fanfare, we got to Colville and ate breakfast, but that is when our boring trip ended.

A man walked in the restaurant looking for a meal and a ride to Spokane. My friend being the kind soul that she was said we would buy him a meal and give him a ride.

He was a skinny guy, maybe early twenties. When he sat down across the table from us, we smelled him immediately. He reeked of beer, cigarettes, and body odor.

We both looked at each other and knew we had messed up. There was no way we were going to be able to give him a ride to Spokane. We were in a single cab pickup and it was raining.

He told us his girlfriend was pregnant and wanted to get married but he wanted to be free so he left.

After we finished our meal, we bought him one. I excused myself to go to the bathroom, and my friend followed. Once inside we turned to each other.

"Okay, how do we get rid of him?" I asked.

"My thoughts exactly." She said.

We figured we could go out the back door to our pickup, jump in, and just drive away.

The plan sounded good. We opened the bathroom door and looked over to where we were seated. To our surprise, he was gone.

We ducked back into the bathroom.

"Maybe he found another ride." She said.

"Not likely." I mustered.

We opened the door and ran for our pickup, jumped in, backed up, and took off down the road with him in the distant past or so we thought.

We joked and laughed about him all the way through the next two towns. About sixty miles later, we pulled into a gas station for fuel.

I went inside to buy some gum and looked back out to where my friend stood filling up the pickup. I watched in horror as she jumped back, and even through the glass windows, I could hear her scream. The man from the restaurant stood up in the back of the pickup and smiled.

I dropped the gum on the floor and ran outside. I yelled profanities at him and he just smiled. He told us that he had been offered rides before and then the people take off on him. This time he said he was going to make sure we did not get away.

To our luck, a police officer pulled into the station and right up to us. It seems the store clerk called him. He let us drive away as he stood next to the man. Wow! What else odd could happen in one day?

Plenty, we soon learned. When we arrived at the grocery store we noticed a young girl, maybe thirteen years old sitting outside.

We did our grocery shopping and when we were leaving the store, we noticed the girl was still there, in front of the store, sitting on the curb.

We stopped and watched as she approached person after person asking for money. An older man stepped from the store beside us with a case of beer and a small bag full of groceries.

We overheard as the young girl approached the man and asked for money. The man asked what she would do for his money. She looked tired, wet, and sad.

"For three hundred dollars I will do whatever you want." We listened in horror as the man accepted her offer and she followed him to his truck.

Without thinking, I yelled. "I will give you three hundred and fifty dollars." The girl turned and looked at me.

The man looked mad. "Three seventy five."

"Four hundred." I only had five hundred dollars with me.

The man was so enraged he dropped his beer. The cans hit the concrete sent explosions of beer mist and foam everywhere.

"What do you want with her?" He demanded.

"What do you want with her is more to the question." I said.

"She offered, I accepted, I have done nothing wrong." He said.

"Shall we ask the police?" I said.

The man turned tail and lit for his truck. The girl walked over to us.

"Why are you out here asking for money?" I asked.

"I followed my boyfriend to Washington and then he dumped me. I am trying to get back home to my mother and father in Missouri." She said.

"How old are you?" My friend asked.

"Twelve." She said.

"How old was your boyfriend?" We asked.

"Nineteen." She answered.

Three hundred dollars is what she said a bus ticket home would cost. We took her to the airport, bought her a plane ticket, and gave her some cab money to get her home from the airport.

I gave her my address and told her that if she got a chance we would like to know that she got home okay. Both of our monthly checks were almost gone, so without stopping at the tack store we went home.

We had some wild adventures with the outside world as we called it then. On that day, we learned not to pick up hitchhikers and that auctions aren't just for cattle.

Our real life lesson came two months later. A letter came with no return address. Inside there were two letters; one from the young girl and the other from her mother thanking us for what we did.

However, I think the most amazing thing was the check from the young girl who stated she had worked two whole months babysitting and mowing lawns to get enough money to pay us back.

The Border

This is one of those stories I haven't told a lot of people. In fact, my parents probably have never even heard this one.

I was nineteen and in Canada, that is the legal drinking age. A couple of my friends and I would go up, drink, play pool, and then come home at midnight.

One night, when we went to cross the border, the American guard told us that we couldn't go up to drink any more. He said they were not going to allow us to cross. My friends waited for a week before they tried again. I didn't go, I was afraid of getting caught. They called me from the bar and said they made it.

I still didn't want to try it, but I did want to go up and have fun with them, so I saddled my horse and headed out. It took me about two hours to get there. When I did, we partied for a couple hours then I saddled up and headed back home as if I had never been there. We did that on many nights until we turned twenty-one.

I felt like a real old time cowboy in one of those old westerns going across the Mexican border for whatever reason and then coming back in the darkness of the night. Everyone used to make fun of me for riding my horses over the border and back again.

When I was younger there used to be a produce stand across the border that used to carry great apples. My horse and I would walk on over get an apple and a drink and head back home again.

The produce was always eaten before we hit the border. I don't know what they would have done if they would have caught me.

Nowadays, I wouldn't even think about it considering all of the Border Security, but back then it was part of life. To me Canada never seemed like another country, it was just the closest town.

Little Boy Green

Well my parents were known to bring home a few unwanted kids every now and then from the local Job Core. It was one such boy who decided to live with us for a year. We never liked each other. I was fourteen and my brother had just left for college.

On his first day, he said to treat him just like a brother. Obviously, he didn't know how my brother and I treated each other. Therefore, I took him literally, and that is how I treated him from that moment on.

In the spring, he tried to ride my horses and when they didn't do what he wanted. He got off punched them, dropped the reins, and headed to the house. He often left the horses in the field with the saddles and bridles still on.

In the summer months, he proceeded to mess up my haystacks by throwing bales in holes or not stacking the hay tight.

When my friends came over to go swimming, he wanted to go along, only to try drowning us in the river. When it came time for the Fair he wanted to ride in the rodeo like I did.

He always slept in the barn, on a pile of hay with a couple blankets and a pillow. He said, "That was the way he liked it." Then he told me I wasn't allowed in our barn when he wasn't there, and if he was there, I had to knock and get permission to enter.

One day he pointed a gun at a passing motorist. From that day on he and I butted heads.

We had a bunch of chickens that laid eggs all over the barn and ranch. Sometimes we found the eggs before they turned rotten.

One day he chucked an egg at me, and when it hit my back, I could tell at once, it was rotten. So, I did what he asked, I treated him like he was my brother. When he went to the house for supper I snuck down, grabbed about ten of those rotten eggs, and made my way to the barn.

I snuck in without knocking and made my way straight to his bed. I shoved all those eggs under his pillow, inside his pillowcase. I snuck out of the barn just as silently as I came in and went up to the house for supper. I took my seat between Mom and Dad at the table and glared across the table at him. He glared back and the hate was evident between us.

"So what happened today?" Mom asked.

"Oh nothing much, we found a nest of rotten eggs." I said.

"I hope you carried them over the hill and got rid of them." Mom said.

"No, we didn't." I replied. "But I carried them away." I smiled a sweet smile across the table and I watched his face turn to a look of concern.

After supper, we all sat around and watched a movie. Afterward, he excused himself to go to bed. I went to my room and opened my window.

About and hour later I heard what I had wanted to hear. A loud scream! I am guessing that was when little boy blue turned green from the smell of those rotten eggs breaking under his pillow as he laid down.

Looking back now, I would almost feel bad about this, but he did say to treat him like my brother.

The Hunting Party

I have had guns pulled on me and pointed at me in my life many times over many things. I think as a backwoods country girl who grew up between the border and a lot of drug dealers and corrupt people you expect things to be high energy and a little dangerous.

I have had guns pointed at me over dead cows and live ones. I have even had a gun pointed at me for doing my job as a store clerk. When I worked security, I saw the wrong end of two guns.

Nevertheless, I have never had a gun pointed at me for killing a deer on my own land until I turned sixteen. I had gone out before daylight and found a good spot to sit and wait for the deer to come in. I spent most of daybreak sitting and waiting for it to get light and, at ten minutes to nine, I started crisscrossing back and fourth across our land. I hunted on our land all morning. Around 11:00, I saw a nice three-point whitetail about two hundred-yards on the tree line. I crouched down and took careful aim. He stepped back into the tree line and I figured I was probably not going to see him again. I snuck up the hill and then towards the tree line. I had scarcely gone a hundred-yards when; again, he stepped from the tree line. I crouched down and aimed. He stood still, and I took a shot.

He jumped and headed for the field across the open hillside, heading straight toward our alfalfa fields. I knew at least maybe I was going to be able to see where he laid down. I knew I had hit him hard.

He went about a three hundred-yards and laid down in our alfalfa field. I waited for him to lay his head down. While he was lying there I snuck around within a hundred-yards and sat down and waited until I was sure he was dead.

I saw his head peek up and look at me so I made myself comfortable for the wait. I had just gotten comfortable when guns started blaring from every direction. I ducked for cover and kept my head low as not to get it shot off.

When the guns shots stopped, I peeked up and watched in horror as three men headed out of the tree line across the fence towards my buck. I stood up and took off running towards my deer.

I saw as two of the men took off running towards the deer as well. I sped up and so did they. I knew it was going to be very close as to who reached the deer first. One of the men yelled for me to leave his deer alone and another yelled he was going to call the police if I touched his deer.

I reached into my back pocket and retrieved my tag. Besides the fact that they had shot a deer that was on our property and were now trespassing, I knew I was in the right for those two facts and the other fact that I was the one that shot the deer in the first place.

I reached the deer and quickly tied my tag to his horn when the first of the three men reached me.

"What the heck do you think you are doing?" He asked me.

"Tagging my deer." I said.

"Your deer! My arse." He said as he started to accuse me of trespassing on his property even though it was my parent's alfalfa field.

"Your property?" I said. "This is my parent's field."

"Bull." The second man said as he reached us. "I have permission to hunt this place."

That I knew to be a lie as my Dad was a big hunter and he hated other people on his land.

"Lie to someone who don't know a shit." I said. "This is my parent's land and you assholes have no right to be here."

"You can't keep us from our deer." The first man said as he reached down and ripped my tag off the deer.

"Your tag!" I screamed. "That is pure shit and you know it. I shot that deer and was waiting for him to die when you three jerks open fired on him."

"You lie." The third and fatter man said. When he reached us, he was out of breath and sounding like a freight train.

"You guys need to get off our land. Now!" I said as forcefully as I could muster.

"Maybe you should run on home before something bad happens to you." The fattest man said. I looked at the three men and realized that maybe I wasn't in the best spot in my life.

"You touch me and my Dad will kill you." I said.

"First, he would have to find us." The first man said.

"He would find you and cut off the protruding parts of you anatomy if you do anything to me." I said.

"Again," the first man said, "he would have to find us."

"Or what's left of you." The third man said. I realized the situation had just gone from bad to deadly when I saw him raise his riffle to belly height and point it straight at me.

I have never been known to be a dumb woman I know when I am outnumbered and right then I felt like Custer at his last stand. I just wish I had Comanche so I could climb on and ride away.

I backed up about four steps when I noticed the three men were preoccupied with something behind me. I thought it might have been a trick to get me to turn around so I never looked.

I figured I suddenly might have had the upper hand so I raised my rifle up to face them and watched in complete satisfaction as they backed up and turned around and made a quick retreat.

I knelt down, retied my tag to the deer's antler, and suddenly felt a nudge.

I turned and found our big black bull behind me. He was big and scary but he was friendly. We had recently had problems with him jumping the fence and crawling into our alfalfa fields. My Dad was about to sell him because of the fact he had no respect for fences. However, at that moment I was glad he liked me and loved alfalfa.

I could still see the men at the edge of the field and I realized that they must have been city boys, a fact that I am very grateful for.

Shortly after this happened I came up with a sign for our property, it read in big bold letters.

If you cross this field, you had better be able to do it in 9.5 seconds, because my bull can do it in 10 flat.

The End

About the Author

Dawn Nelson is true cowgirl. She was born and raised on a cattle ranch in North-Eastern Washington state. Married to a cattle rancher she now calls Creston, Washington her home.

Dawn, her husband Kris, and their daughter Laren own and operate a large cattle ranch in central Washington. Dawn enjoys showing her registered cattle, riding horses, camping, hunting, and other outdoor activities. She also volunteers a lot of her time to 4-H and is actively involved in her county Cattlemen's Association.